AN EVERLASTING LOVE AFFAIR

The Story of Lou and Irene Candela

Lou Candela

authorHOUSE®

AuthorHouse™
1663 Liberty Drive
Bloomington, IN 47403
www.authorhouse.com
Phone: 1-800-839-8640

First published by AuthorHouse 11/28/2011

ISBN: 978-1-4520-1108-0 (sc)
ISBN: 978-1-4520-1107-3 (hc)
ISBN: 978-1-4520-1106-6 (ebk)

Library of Congress Control Number: 2010904826

Printed in the United States of America

Table of Contents

Photos

Coming to America

You probably are looking at the cover of this book and asking yourselves, "What is this story all about?"

First, let me introduce myself. My name is Lou Candela. The reason I am writing this book is that throughout my adult years, whenever I have engaged people in conversation about my life, they always ask how I met my wife, Irene. After hearing my story, almost all of them suggest that I have had an interesting life and I should write a book. So here it is.

My pop's parents, Antonio Candela and Beatrice Santoro Candela, were both born in Naples, Italy and left to come to America in April 1886. They arrived at Ellis Island in New York and settled in lower Manhattan in a section called "Little Italy." It's my understanding that he was a tailor and she was a housewife. They had four children, three boys and one girl. The eldest was Lucy, then Michael, then my pop Milton, and lastly Frank. My pop was born in March 1892.

Life in lower Manhattan at that time was not much to speak highly of. Everyone was just trying to make ends meet … lots of poverty and hard times. When Pop and his siblings were young, both his parents died. I never found out exactly how they died, because in my parents' time, children were never told anything. Everything that went on between my parents was always secret. They would never speak in front of the children. To this day, I can't understand the reasoning for that. I do know that my pop boarded with a Jewish family while growing up, and he did learn to speak a little Yiddish. As a youth, he did whatever it took to survive, and of course that meant swiping fruit and other food from the pushcarts along Mott Street.

My mom's parents, Antonio Corso and Domenica Lombardo Corso, were both born in Sicily. They had five children, three boys and two girls. The eldest was Louis, then Mom, Rose, Salvatore, and lastly Joseph. Mom was born on January 20, 1897. My grandfather Antonio worked on the railroad, and my grandmother was a housewife.

By the time of the First World War, they had a few relatives living in New York, and Louis was eager to join them and start a new life in America. In 1914, my grandfather gave Louis permission to leave Sicily to live with his uncle in New York. In 1915, Grandpa Antonio decided to send the rest of the family to America. Grandma and the children arrived in Ellis Island in New York. At that time, my uncle Lou had his own apartment, and that is where they all settled to live with him. Grandpa Antonio promised he would come the following year. However, he never did come to America. I can only guess why he remained behind. After his family left Sicily, he probably felt free again and may have had second thoughts about reuniting with his wife and children.

By this time, Pop was an auto mechanic and on his own. He met Mom shortly after she arrived in America, and after a one-year courtship, they married in 1916. Within a span of ten years, they had seven children. First was Anthony or Andy, then Charles, Mike, Beatrice, me, Minnie, and lastly Frank. Charles died shortly after birth. Of the six surviving children, I was the fourth child. I was born on July 2, 1922.

At that time, we were living on Sixty-Fifth Street and Amsterdam Avenue in Manhattan, on the third floor of a four-story tenement building. Uncle Lou, his wife Jenny, their children, and our Nona had an apartment in the same building, and since Mom was having children almost every year, Nona was always in our apartment. Naturally, she did not speak English, so all of us children learned Italian or spoke some of the language.

When I was four years old, Pop decided to move us to the Bronx. He bought this old, three-story, wood-frame, attached house on 165th Street and Washington Avenue. The house had no heat and no hot water. There were tenants living on the third floor; however, the second floor was empty ... and that was where our family was to reside. At street level, there was an empty store. Pop somehow thought that by buying this house, he would be able to rent out the store and it would help to pay off the mortgage. A family did rent the store and tried to make a go of it as a small cafeteria. That venture failed shortly afterward, and the store remained empty again.

Although we had neither central heat nor hot water, we had a large black coal stove in the kitchen that had six lids on top to cook on. Mom would remove the round black lids so as to have direct heat from the burning coal, which would heat the food or boil water. Almost all of our time in the winter months was spent in the kitchen because it was the warmest room in the house.

On Saturdays, Mom would fill up as many pots of water as she could, then put them on the stove and let them get really hot. That meant it was time for our baths. Now, at the time, we had only one brand of bath soap, called "O.K. Soap." It was shaped like an octagon and it felt like it weighed two pounds. The color was tan and it did not smell too good, either. The soap felt oily and smelled like bleach. That one soap was used for everything from washing our hands and faces to bathing. Mom also used it when washing clothes with the scrub board in the bathtub. She would be on her knees over the tub scrubbing the clothes with that soap. Things were quite primitive in those days.

First to go into the bathtub were my two sisters, Beatrice and Minnie. When they were through, my brothers Andy and Mike would take their bath. Then last to go were my younger brother Frank and I. By this time, the water was not too clear, nor was it too warm. After we got out of the tub and let the remaining water drain out, you could see two black rings around the entire tub: the upper one from Andy and Mike, and the lower one from Frank and me. If Mom did not get to clean the tub soon afterward, she had a big problem. Once those rings dried on the tub, it was almost impossible to remove them. Poor Mom!

The thing I hated the most was going to bed at night. I wore my pop's old undershirts that had many holes in them caused by moths. I had no undershorts because Mom could not afford them. In the wintertime, the bedrooms were really cold, and after removing my outer clothes, I was left with only Pop's old undershirt and nothing else. Andy and Mike would sleep at the head of the bed, and Frank and I would sleep at the other end. All you could hear was four kids shivering until they warmed up enough to fall asleep. We did this every night throughout the whole winter.

Each morning after waking, we went into the bathroom to wash up for school. When we turned the faucet on, out came frigid water. I would just wet two fingers on each hand and dab my cheeks—that was it. I also had to wet my hair so I could comb it. Since I did not have a hat, either, by the time I arrived at school, my hair was frozen with ice.

In 1929, when I was seven years old, the stock market crashed. That was the beginning of a long, dreadful time for many people throughout the United States. At that time, Pop was still working, so he decided to convert the empty store to an apartment for us. At the same time, he had the contractor add heat and hot water to the entire house. After we moved to our new ground-floor apartment, Pop rented the second floor.

By 1930, there were many apartment buildings that had a lot of vacancies. When a family wanted to rent an apartment, the entire apartment had to be completely painted and in very good condition before anyone would rent it. Here's how it worked: the renters would only sign a one-year lease because it gave them the option of moving out after the year was up. The reason they only rented for one year was that during that period, they never had to take care of the apartment. They never had to clean the walls or floors or keep the apartment in repair. When the year was up, they would leave the messy apartment for a new place that would be neatly painted and cleaned.

After the tenants moved, Pop would go to the paint store and get a gallon of white lead paint and tubes of color that resembled toothpaste tubes. As you can guess, a gallon of white lead paint was very heavy. Once in the empty apartment, Pop would open the gallon can and scoop out a small portion of the white lead into an empty can. Then, after adding a small amount of turpentine, he would stir it until it thinned out to a thick liquid. I would be by his side and he would tell me to thin out the rest of the white lead as he had done. It took almost forever before I had the white lead thinned out enough to be able to paint. Pop would then add the different oil colors from the tubes. When painting an apartment in those days, each room was always a different color, and the wall molding was a different color, too.

This picture was taken around 1928.
Mike is on the left, Mom in the middle, and Andy on the right.
It's the only picture that I have of my brothers as children.
I just had to include it in my story; get a load of those bathing suits!

Most renters preferred to rent in a large apartment building where they knew their fellow tenants from other places. In the summer's hot weather, they could sit out front, talk, and tell stories. At that time, apartments were being rented for twenty-five dollars per month, including gas and electricity.

Later on in the 1930s, Pop lost his job as things were getting tougher for most families because of the Great Depression. His boss felt really bad and offered to take out a second mortgage on our home.

Pop had a hard time getting another job. Finally, during the winter of 1934, he obtained a position as an auto mechanic repairing cars in an open lot for a Chevy dealer. Their garage was small, and Pop had no choice but to work outdoors on the cars. He was earning fifteen dollars a week. It wasn't much, but whatever he brought home helped a lot.

Each night on his way home from work, he stopped at another open lot where there were piles of old, rotted wood. He would put as much of the wood as he could in the backseat of his car. We kids would then unload the wood and put it in the basement to use for firewood during the winter months.

Most people at that time did not have telephones, but my mom's sister, who lived in Brooklyn, had one. The drugstores and candy stores all had telephone booths, which people used to reach their relatives or friends. So when my aunt had to reach my mom, she would call the drugstore on our corner, and the young employee would run a quarter of a block to our house. Mom would then run back to the store to speak with her sister.

On the opposite side of the street from the drugstore was the grocery store, where we would buy all of our groceries. Most families had small, metal quart containers for milk. The grocer had a few large, stainless steel milk containers that held approximately twenty-five gallons of milk. The grocer would lift the lid of his large container and, with a ladle, pour milk into our quart container. The sanitary conditions for the milk were not too healthy since we had no air conditioning in the summer and the grocer would hang flypaper traps all around the ceiling to catch the flies.

Our grocer had one large notebook that contained all the names of his customers. Since we never had money, he would write down the amount of money we spent on groceries under our name in his notebook. Whenever my pop got a few dollars, he would send one of the kids to pay off some of our debt. Believe me, that's how it was for most families. Even the grocer had a hard time making ends meet.

In the second house to the left of us, there was a horse stable beneath the home. Here they boarded all the delivery horses belonging to the milk company that delivered to homes and stores each day. (Delivery cost more money, which is why most families had their own metal milk containers to take to the grocer.) In the second house to our right, there was a blacksmith's stable, also beneath the home. Here the blacksmith would shoe all the horses for the milk company. During the summer, if a horse died in the stable, the owner would have it dragged out to the curb in front of the stable. Believe it or not, the horse could lie there for a week or more before the sanitation department would come and drag it onto a truck and haul it away. Can you imagine in the ninety-degree heat all the flies and other insects on that horse—not to mention the foul odor? Every time a horse died, it was the same routine. It would lie in the street for a week or two before being taken away.

Now, what about my family? We lived between the horse stable and the blacksmith. What do you think we had as guests in our home? I must be honest and tell you we had mice, rats, cockroaches, black beetles, flies, lice, bedbugs, and ants. We also had a small female alley cat. She was great at catching the mice, but when the rats confronted her, she would run away.

We also had dogs from time to time. On my way home from school, I would sometimes see a pack of dogs walking toward me, and I would call them over to me. Almost all of them would continue walking past me, but usually one or two of them would come to me. In those days, many people owned dogs, and if they could not afford to keep them, they would let the dogs go astray. Also, there were no laws requiring people to keep dogs on a leash. When a dog is loose and sees other dogs, he will join the pack and never go back home. Still, occasionally a dog did come when I called and followed me home. That's the way we always acquired our dogs. Sometimes these dogs would stay with us for a while, but usually, since they were not on a leash, they would take off and join the pack as soon as they saw other strays.

We did have one dog that stayed with us for many years. He was a beautiful spitz and a really loveable dog. All too often, though, when we had a dog at home, he would get out and get hit or killed by a car. Every time that happened, all of us kids would sit on the edge of our bed and cry.

As youngsters during the summer months, we got free milk and bread from our public schools each day. That helped a lot. When my oldest brother Andy was fourteen years old, he worked for Postal Telegraph delivering letters on foot. He received one penny for each letter he delivered, and that was in Manhattan. They would give him between five and ten letters. As soon as he delivered them, he ran back to the center and waited his turn for the next few letters. That's how it was in those times; we were not alone in trying to make ends meet. The entire United States was in the same, if not worse, condition we were in.

Mom had a hard time with her four boys. For example, when we were asked to go buy groceries, we preferred to go play ball with our friends. As a rule, it was difficult for Mom to get us to stay at home and help with chores around the house. I remember Mom chasing me with the broom, and I would run into the backyard and climb up the clothesline pole. Of course, Mom would yell up at me, "Wait 'til your father gets home!" When Pop came home from work at night, Mom would tell him what we had done that day, and that's when the beatings would start. Off came his belt, and when he was finished, we sounded like a bunch of wolves howling away in unison. We never learned from this because it happened quite regularly.

When Andy was eighteen years old, he bought a 1929 Ford with a rumble seat. He paid twenty-five dollars for it. (New cars were selling for approximately five hundred dollars at the time.) On one summer day, Andy told me that we were going to get some corn upstate. It was

1934, and I was twelve years old. I had no idea what he was up to. Andy was very daring and would attempt almost anything.

We drove up to a farm outside of Brewster, New York. Andy took a sack out of the car and we walked to the cornstalks in the field. We had started filling up the sack with corn when the owner of the farm spotted us from a distance and ran toward us. Andy grabbed the sack and said, "Let's get the heck out of here!" We ran and jumped over a stone wall, only to land in bushes with large thorns on them. I started screaming and Andy told me, "Be quiet or the farmer will see us, and we'll probably be arrested!"

We lay in the bushes for quite some time before Andy thought it was safe to get back into the car. We managed to bring a little corn home, but we were all cut up and bleeding on our arms, legs, and faces. What an adventure!

As young boys, all we played were street games. If one boy owned a baseball bat, glove, and ball, he was our idol, and we were thrilled when he would play with us. Some of the boys owned old gloves and that was all they had. Some of us owned nothing at all. When the cover of a baseball peeled off, we would tape it all around with black electrical tape. This made the ball much heavier, and if it hit you, it hurt a lot.

Many of the games we played were "homemade" games like stickball, box-ball, and stoop-ball. For example, stickball is played similarly to baseball, in the middle of a city street. A manhole cover would be home plate. First and third base would be the fenders of parked cars on opposite sides of the street. Second base would be a second manhole cover. The bat would be the handle of a broomstick, and the ball would be a pink Spalding rubber ball. Since we did not have any money to buy sports equipment, we had lots of fun with just a Spalding ball. That made us quite content.

We learned to make the best of what we had when we played sports. When we played football in the street and a car ran over the ball and crushed it, we would unstitch the football, take the central tube out, fill up the ball with newspaper, make it as tight as possible, and thread the leather stitching back on. Then we were ready to play again.

As kids, we would do some crazy things. There was one street that had a large hill and then straightened out at the center of the block. My brothers Andy and Mike had an old car tire at the top of this hill, and since I was small enough to fit inside the tire, I had no choice when they told me to get in. Once inside, they promised me that they would be on either side of me as they rolled the tire down the hill.

But when the tire (with me in it) started to roll down the hill, my brothers could not keep up with it. There I was, spinning and spinning and holding on for dear life to the inner rim with my fingers. Then the tire veered off to the right side of the hill and hit the curb. The tire and I went flying. The next thing I knew, my arms, legs, face, and body were full of cuts and bruises, my shirt and pants were all ripped, and I had no idea where I was because I was quite dizzy from going around and around. Along came Andy and Mike. They were somewhat worried and just happy that I survived the ordeal.

At that point, the three of us were afraid to go home. When we arrived, Mom took one look at the three of us and got the broom. First Mom beat us, and then when Pop came home from work, he automatically took the belt off his trousers and hit the three of us until we were all moaning and crying. Again I must repeat, being boys, we always did things we weren't supposed to do, and of course suffered the consequences. Believe me, we were strapped very often.

Another thing we did as children was build scooters out of roller skates and the wagons from baby carriages. The problem with the scooters was that the skate wheels were very small, and if you went over a crack in the sidewalk, you'd go flying out of the scooter and land right on your face.

Whenever a house in the neighborhood had a fire and the house became uninhabitable, we kids took our wagons to the empty house. We stripped all the plumbing—brass, copper, and lead pipes—throughout the house. We put it all in our wagons and headed straight for the junkyard. After unloading our loot to the junk man, he would give us maybe twenty-five cents for the whole works. We kids took whatever he gave us and split it up among ourselves. Then we would return to the same burned-out house and start stripping all the siding and whatever wood we could carry in our wagons to bring home as firewood. There were many children and adults doing this, as firewood was hard to find. Within a few weeks, everything from the house would be gone.

At school, I was just an average student. I did enjoy arithmetic and spelling, as I was pretty good at those two subjects. There were two other subjects that I could not handle at all: geography and history. I did very poorly in them.

After the sixth grade, I was sent to a junior high school, where I chose to take industrial courses. There, we were given shop classes every afternoon, plus a little math, spelling, history, or geography. Our shop classes included carpentry, machine shop, and sheet metal. I took courses in all of them. My brother Andy at this time had a small shop for repairing and refinishing autos, and I thought I would be able to work with him. The problem was that in the 1930s, no one had any money to get their cars repaired. Andy was forced to close his shop.

When I left school in the ninth grade, I decided to go to a vocational school, but I left a few months later because I had to go to work and help out the family. During the 1930s, there were many employment agencies in Manhattan along Sixth Avenue from Twentieth Street to Twenty-Sixth Street. At street level, they had large billboards where they would place small, three-by-five-inch cards saying "Man Wanted" or "Boy Wanted." The problem was that there were thousands of men applying for whatever job they could get. Most jobs at that time started at twenty-five cents an hour.

I myself did not have much luck. I would go downtown every day and end up with nothing. I did get a job for a brief time in a picture-frame factory, and then a few more hit-and-run jobs. Finally, I landed one where they manufactured costume jewelry. The company was called Select Jewelry. I worked there from 1939 to 1941.

At that time, most people working in factories and office buildings got paid every Friday. Each employee would receive a small, tan envelope with their wages inside. All wages were in cash. When my brothers and sisters arrived home from work on Friday evening, my mom would sit us all around the kitchen table and, one by one, ask us for our pay envelopes. Andy was first. Mom would open the envelope, count the money, and slide a quarter over to Andy. That was his allowance for the week. Next came Mike. After opening his envelope, she counted his money and slid a quarter to him. Then came Beatrice, me, and Minnie. We each received a quarter for the week. After receiving our twenty-five cents, we would spend it at the movie theater. None of us complained, because the times were tough, and whatever we could give Mom and Pop helped a lot.

The Draft

In 1940, the United States started the draft for young men over twenty-one years old for military duty of one year's duration. Defense plants were sprouting throughout the country. On December 7, 1941, with the Japanese attack on Pearl Harbor, American involvement in World War II began. It was to be a big change for our entire family and for all of the United States of America.

Andy was twenty-five years old, but when he was a child, he had cut his hand and fingers on some glass, and the army classified him as unfit for duty. Next there was Mike at age twenty-two. He was called to service two months after the war started. They shipped him out to Australia immediately, the reason being that the Japanese were threatening to invade Australia. Frank at that time was fifteen years old and still in school. Since I was only nineteen, I needed parental consent to join up, but Mom refused to sign papers allowing me to enlist in the army.

So I left my job with the jewelry manufacturer and started to work for the government in a defense plant. My working hours at the defense plant were from 6:30 p.m. 'til 6:00 a.m., with a half hour for lunch. I worked eleven hours a night, five nights a week. The factory made submarine and battleship parts in cast iron and aluminum. They weighed between twenty and forty pounds each. As these parts came from the machine shop, my job was to dip them in a fifty-five gallon drum of carbon tetrachloride to clean all the oil from the parts. Then I sprayed them with zinc chromate paint and baked them in large ovens for two hours at 250 degrees. Then I sprayed two coats of battleship-gray enamel on them, baking again between each coat. The finished product looked like porcelain.

There was only one problem with my job. In those days, if they even knew, they did not tell us that carbon tetrachloride could kill you. Each night, there were many metal parts that had to be degreased. When I opened the cover of the fifty-five gallon drum of carbon tetrachloride to clean the parts, I gagged and had trouble breathing. Every night, it was same routine. Slowly and surely, the chemical was making me sick, and I was having trouble breathing. When I arrived home each morning after working all night, feeling sick from inhaling the fumes, I would beg my mom to let me quit that job and join the army. But there was no way whatsoever Mom would let me quit that job. Money was more important, and I had no choice but to continue at that plant. The thought of inhaling those fumes each night was something I had to live with. It was true, though: money was an important factor for my mom and pop. I knew I was helping with the family's financial problems, but slowly it did begin to affect my health.

After a few months, I went to the army recruiting station in Manhattan and obtained the forms necessary to join the army. I wanted to volunteer, but my mom still refused to sign the papers. Within the next few months, I brought another form for Mom to sign. She said, "Sooner or later, the army will call you. Don't be in any hurry."

In 1942, the government lowered the draft age to twenty. So when I turned twenty, I received my draft card, and toward the end of the year, I finally got called to service. Oh, happy day! It was an honor to be part of a vast undertaking to help the US government.

Army Life

I reported for duty at Penn Station in December 1942 and was sent by train to Fort Dix, New Jersey. At that time of year, it was very cold. I remember the first morning at Fort Dix. They put the lights on at 5:00 a.m. and yelled for us recruits to get dressed and fall out in ten minutes. I remember there was a private first class who was going to teach us new recruits how to march. It was ridiculous! But they were trying to let us know what the army was about. Also during my first day, we were ordered to the supply room, where we received our army clothing and were told to ship our civilian clothes back home. On my second morning at Fort Dix, same routine, up at 5:00 a.m., at ten minutes after five we were again attempting to march, pitch black outside, fifteen degrees … and I said, "So this is the army!?"

After three days at Fort Dix, we boarded trains for warmer climates. We knew we were going south since the temperatures were going up. Approximately a day later, we ended up at Fort Jackson, South Carolina. They were forming a new infantry division. Here they would put approximately fifteen thousand recruits together, and we would be called the One Hundredth Infantry Division. Lucky me, I ended up in the field artillery. An infantry division had three infantry regiments and artillery support. I became one of a crew of eight men on a 105mm howitzer. Four guns made up our battery, which included one hundred men altogether. That was the beginning of my three and a half years in the army.

After basic training was done for the day, we GIs gathered at the PX every evening and sat around a large table. All my buddies ordered many glasses of beer, and they all smoked. I in turn ordered a milk shake, and I did not smoke. The reason for this was that my pop would light up a cigarette every morning as soon as he woke up. After a minute or so, he would start gagging. He had trouble breathing, of course. He was a chain smoker and always had a cigarette in his hand. When we were young kids growing up, he would hold up his cigarette and say, "This can kill you." I knew one thing; it surely wasn't helping him. After witnessing this, I decided I would never smoke. My pop never drank alcohol. That was good. We kids also never touched hard liquor.

Even so, I would have a good time with my buddies, and we would spend a great evening together. Yes, this would go on every evening during training. Although my buddies drank and smoked, it did not mean that I had to do the same to enjoy their company. I didn't care what they did. I knew what I had to do. So there I was in the army, enjoying a milk shake while my buddies got drunk every evening. Who was the smart one?

As a rule, we GIs got along very well in basic training at Fort Jackson. But there was one soldier I had a problem with during this time. He was a real country boy from the south. His name was Abner. He was tall and really strong, and what you might call a bully. First off, he complained about being in the artillery. He said our outfit was too chicken for him. He always talked about transferring to the paratroopers to be with "real men." I did not like his constant complaining or his attitude.

One Sunday morning around 7:00 a.m. and after being out all Saturday night, he came into the barracks with another GI. Both were still reeling from drinking all night. Abner then approached the bunk of a sleeping GI and proceeded to piss on the face of this unfortunate GI. The soldier woke up yelling, which in turn woke us all up. I heard what had happened, and I approached the two drunks and confronted them about their behavior. Abner then said to me, "Candela, if you would like a piece of my ass, then let's go outside and see if you can get it!" That was the first time I'd heard that turn of phrase. It wasn't used in New York, but in the south it was common when two men wanted to rumble. Of course I knew better than to go outside. I didn't stand a chance against the both of them. They threatened to assault me. I just ignored them and walked away.

As a rule, the southern boys did not care for the boys from the north. For them, the Civil War was still deep in their thoughts. These two bullies had been drinking and were feeling tough. They decided to let us know that we were in their neck of the woods, and pissed on a very helpless New York Jewish boy because he could not defend himself. I knew in the future I had to be very careful with these two bullies.

A few weeks later, we GIs were washing up after morning chow. While all the sinks were occupied, in comes Abner with his towel over his shoulder. He automatically pushed a soldier away from a sink to use it himself. Unfortunately for Abner, he did not realize that we had a former heavyweight boxer from Massachusetts named Jerry. He happened to be at another sink and saw the whole incident. Jerry grabbed Abner by the shoulder, turned him around, and punched him right on the jaw, knocking him down on his butt. The boxer warned Abner to never mistreat defenseless solders again. I congratulated Jerry and thanked him for standing up to that moron. I wish I could have done it, but I do not think I was capable of it. What a great feeling it was to see Abner sitting on his ass!

After months of training, we were ordered to Tennessee for winter maneuvers. The weather was miserable, rainy, and cold. We went straight from maneuvers in Tennessee to Fort Bragg, North Carolina. The army decided to use our division as a replacement depot. They took GIs from our infantry division as needed to replace GIs in other divisions who were combat casualties. In turn, as our division lost our boys, they had to be replaced with new recruits. We had to teach the recruits and continue this army lifestyle until we became battle ready and could be called whenever they needed an entire division.

The word finally came that we were shipping out. Before we went overseas, though, all the GIs had to be given a physical and dental checkup so as to be in good health when we left the United States. When the army dentist saw my teeth, he told me that he would have to fill all my back teeth. I sat in that chair for a few hours and must have pushed his hand from my mouth many times. When he was finished, I had no feeling and could not talk because my tongue was numb. It took almost a week before I could speak and eat properly.

Our division went to Camp Shanks, New York prior to leaving for Europe. I was able to get passes to leave the base and visit my parents in Brooklyn. They had moved from the Bronx in 1943 as the neighborhood where we had lived changed dramatically. Andy was married and living in Queens. Mike was with the army in the Pacific Theater of Operations. Beatrice and Minnie were also married and away from home. Frank was in the navy in the Pacific theater as well. It was nice to come home to see Mom and Pop. I didn't have a steady girl to go see; I had just dated from time to time. There was no way I could ask a girl out with the allowance that I received from Mom. It wasn't easy to make and spend for good times. However, I always enjoyed the company of women. I have often said that women are the most beautiful of God's creations.

About a week before my division departed for France, we were issued rubber combat boots. Because there were not enough boots to go around, I volunteered to give mine up to an infantryman who had not received a pair. I was told I would receive a new pair before we left for Europe. There I was thinking I was being a good soldier and volunteering to give up my boots, knowing I would get another pair. A few days later, I did in fact get a new pair. I wear a size nine and a half shoe, and the only size they had left was a thirteen. Yup, I got stuck with them. I thought, "Lou, when are you going to learn that you never volunteer for anything in this man's army?"

Finally, in October 1944, we went overseas and landed in Marseille, France. Here we became part of the US Seventh Army.

During the first few weeks of combat, my chief of section volunteered to go up front with the forward observers. I was the gunner corporal of our gun crew, and after he left, I became the chief of section for the remainder of the war. We went through the Vosges Mountains in northeast France. We continued to the Maginot line and seized Fort Schiesseck. It was a fourteen-story-deep fortress with twelve-foot thick, steel-reinforced concrete walls. Unbelievable!

When I entered the fort and saw how big it was, I was somewhat inquisitive. There were staircases going down on every floor, with many rooms for the soldiers to bunk. I decided to go down and look around. When I had walked down four flights and looked at the rooms on each floor, I decided to go back up again. I was a little nervous being there all by myself. I walked up each flight very quietly and felt much relief when I arrived at the top.

By this time, I was having some problems with my captain's behavior. In general, our four howitzers were placed in an open field outside the villages we occupied. The weather was cold: snow, rain, and mud. Every time we advanced to a new position, we had to dig foxholes regardless of how deep the snow was. One problem with that was that the ground was frozen at least a foot deep. In one instance, we were moving along at 3:00 a.m. to a new position. After setting up the howitzers in an open field, the word came down to dig in. The men were cold, wet, and tired. I instructed them to take the tarp off the truck and lay it on the snow. I told the boys to sleep on top of the tarp as best they could. And where do you think my captain was? In a nice, warm house on the edge of the village, getting drunk and having fun with the locals. This he did regularly.

The next morning, he checked our gun position and saw that I had not attempted to dig in as all the other gun sections had. (They did not make much headway.) Right then and there, he berated me and threatened to have me taken up front with the forward observers and have my head blown off. And that's the truth! He questioned me about not digging the foxholes as he had ordered. I tried to explain to him that the ground was frozen and it was almost impossible to accomplish this duty. He then said to me, "Candela, when I give an order, I expect you to carry it out!" Then he went on about me being the only soldier who didn't do as he commanded. How could I have told my men to dig in during this cold night at 3:00 a.m. with two feet of snow on the ground?

During another move to a new position one night, we placed the four guns in an open field outside a small village. My captain, of course, was in a nice, warm house getting drunk as usual and partying with the mademoiselles. The next morning, he came to lay the four guns. That's an army term that means to face the guns toward the enemy's position using surveying equipment and panoramic scopes. The army would give our officers aerial reconnaissance photos of the entire region, and when laying our guns, the forward observers, who had the same photos, would calculate approximately where the shells would hit their targets.

So there was the captain, pie-eyed drunk and still floating from the night before, coming to lay the guns. He had the guns facing the wrong way, and I said to the lieutenant, "Sir, the captain is drunk and he doesn't know what he's doing."

The lieutenant replied, "Candela, don't you say another word."

I said, "Sir, if we have to fire a mission, we may harm our own soldiers."

Well, after the captain left, the lieutenant re-laid the guns, and everything was back to normal. I couldn't understand how the junior officers put up with his drunkenness. I myself thought he was a great liability to the troops, and that's why I had no respect for him.

In the winter of 1944, I was having lots of problems with my feet. Wearing a size thirteen combat boot on a size nine and a half foot didn't help too much. I wore two pairs of socks, and during the day when I was very active, my socks would get wet from the heat of my rubber boots. Then at night, my socks would get really cold. My feet would feel numb.

One day, there were approximately ten American soldiers who had just been killed. All were lying side by side with their combat boots neatly lined up next to their bodies. When a GI dies in combat, a feeling of helplessness goes through your mind. After a while, though, you just accept it. That was why, when I looked for a pair of boots from the soldiers who had just been killed, the emotion was not as bad. All I wanted was a pair that fit, and here was my chance. I approached the first pair and tried them on: too big. After trying on three or four pairs, I finally found a pair that felt good. I, in turn, left my boots by the dead soldier and thanked the fallen hero.

Lou on top of an army truck

Lou – France, 1944

Paris

After Paris was liberated by our troops in 1944, commanders would hand-pick soldiers from their outfits for rest and recreation in Paris. One day, my lieutenant came to me and said. "Candela, you're getting a three-day pass to Paris. Go to the supply sergeant, get a new uniform, and be ready to leave within one hour." What a great feeling it was. I boarded a truck with the other soldiers from different outfits, and we were on our way to Paris.

Upon arriving at the hotel, entering my room, and looking around, I saw a nice, soft bed with clean sheets. Next I entered the bathroom, and there it was … a bathtub. I started to fill it up with hot water, and when it was half full, I stripped down and sat in that hot tub for a long time, occasionally adding hot water. Boy, that felt good.

Next, I dressed up in my new uniform and was ready to go out and explore Paris. There were many young mademoiselles waiting in front of the hotel, and as I exited the lobby onto the sidewalk, here they came. I still remember what they said. "*Allo*, baby. Come with me, baby." They grabbed me by the arm and away we went. This went on for the most part of my leave. Like the song says, "Heaven, I'm in heaven!"

When I arrived back with my outfit, all the GIs asked me if I had seen the Eiffel Tower or Notre Dame Cathedral. I just said "What Eiffel Tower? What cathedral?" Then they asked me what I did the whole time in Paris. My answer was, "Three days of *ooh la la*."

Remember Abner, the country bully I met in basic training? Here's what happened to him at about this time. During our first days in combat, the Germans shelled our position and we all ran for our foxholes. All, that is, except Abner, our tough guy. He was so frightened that he was running all around and apparently did not even think of jumping into the foxhole. After seeing this, I decided to remind him of all the things he had bragged about while in the States. After that, he was really pissed off at me.

One morning as I was walking up a hill going to the mess truck for chow, guess who was standing at the top of the hill with a rifle in his hand? Yup, it was Abner. He had the rifle pointed right at me. He was drunk again and told me he had had enough crap from me. He was about twenty feet from me, and took a shot. The bullet went above my head. I had my rifle over my shoulder, but I did not dare take it down. Again he took a shot at me, and again the bullet went over my head. By this time, a few of the other GIs were able to take away his rifle. When I went up to him, I told him I intended to keep my eye on him, and I walked away to the chow truck.

Why didn't I report this incident? Usually when there was a confrontation between soldiers, they would settle it among themselves. We tried not to let the officers know what was going on.

Not too long after this incident, we were getting shelled pretty hard. As usual, we all managed to get to our foxholes except for Abner. He ended up getting wounded and was taken to the field hospital. It was the last I ever saw him. He never came back to our outfit. I must say, it is dangerous to put a gun into the hands of a frustrated drunk. We were all very lucky.

In December 1944, a memorandum came down from headquarters asking for volunteers to parachute into Bastogne. This was to reinforce our troops, who were surrounded by the Germans. My captain asked me if I would like to volunteer. I think he was looking to get rid of me for good. My thinking was, "First of all, I have never been in a plane. Second, they would have to put me into the parachute, hook me up, and push me out of the plane, because I would never jump out of it on my own."

My answer to the captain was, "Sir, as long as it's not an order, I would rather stay here with my outfit." He was not too happy with me or my answer. But I never went to Bastogne.

On one occasion after moving to a new position, I spotted a young, stray dog that was haggard and hungry looking. He was a German shepherd, and I had always liked that breed. I enticed him over with some K-ration biscuits, which were more suitable for dogs than for us GIs anyway. After a few days of feeding and taking care of him, he stayed by my side. I called him Lucky.

Let me explain the reason behind the name. During our first days of combat in France, and after a gun battle with the enemy, there would be dead horses in the villages' streets. At this time, the Germans had some horse-drawn artillery wagons, and naturally after a battle there would be some dead horses, too. After all the shooting ended, civilians would come out with knives and saws to carve up the horses for food. The first time I saw this, I was taken aback by it, but when you're hungry and have no food, any meat will do. For that reason, you did not see too many dogs or cats around the villages, either. So when I saw Lucky, this young stray German shepherd, I knew he was really lucky, and I was glad he stayed with me.

During one of our advances, after laying the guns, we spotted a small bunker that the Germans had had to leave because we were approaching the area. They had tried to blow it up, but we managed to clear the entrance. To our surprise, it was large enough to hold about ten men comfortably.

Again, let me explain how it was at that time. There were eight men to each howitzer, and every night there were four men who could sleep and four men who had to guard the gun's position. Guard duty started at 10:00 p.m. and ended up at 6:00 a.m. the following morning. Meanwhile, the other four men would sleep unless there was a fire mission.

Because the former German bunker was near our position, that's where we decided to bunk. I brought Lucky in with me. All the other GIs started to bitch and complain. They didn't want a smelly dog sharing our bunker. There we were, all of these men who hadn't bathed, hadn't changed their underwear or stockings in weeks, and smelled as bad as some of the toilets you find at today's gas stations, and they were complaining about a dog. I told them the dog stays, and that's final.

For the first time in a few weeks, some of the GIs removed their rubber boots. You can imagine the horrible smell that came from their socks; steam could even be seen coming out of the socks as well. There is a TV commercial today of a man sitting in a lounge chair and removing his shoes. His dog sitting next to him rolls over and faints after getting a whiff of his socks. That's how bad the scene in the bunker was. I'm surprised Lucky didn't pass out, too.

As the soldiers were removing their socks, one GI was having trouble getting his off. He noticed a brown spot on one sock. As he was removing it, he saw there was dried blood on his heel. When he finally got his sock off, the blood started to flow. There was a small piece of shrapnel protruding from his skin. I called the medic, and after looking at the wound, the medic removed the shrapnel, cleaned his ankle, and bandaged it up. The GI was then up and ready to go. Not a bad way to earn a Purple Heart. And it wasn't all that unusual; there were times during the cold winter of 1944 when GIs would get more seriously wounded and never even feel the injury because their body parts were too cold.

We were at this position only a few days before leaving for a village closer to Germany. After we had laid the guns and dug our foxholes, we didn't realize it, but the German forward observers spotted our position and ordered the German artillery to fire. Usually artillerymen fire their first few rounds just to zero in on their target. Once they accomplish this, they then fire for effect. This resulted in a barrage of artillery shells into our position. As the shells started to come at us, I jumped into my foxhole, calling Lucky and trying to get him in the hole with me. The shelling got pretty heavy, and he got so frightened that he started running toward the woods. That was the last time I saw him. I had become very attached to him; I felt secure having him with me. I only hope someone found him and took care of him, so he did not become someone's meal.

The End Is in Sight

During the winter of 1944-45, we were in the field all the time, with lots of snow on the ground and cold weather. Most of the guys did not bathe too often. When we felt dirty, we were sometimes able to take our helmets, fill them with snow, and melt the snow over the fires that were burning to help keep us warm. When the water was warm enough, you could strip down really fast, wash as best you could all over, and quickly get dressed again. Doing this from time to time helped you feel much better—and a lot cleaner for it, too.

In January 1945, we went through the Saverne Pass in the plains of Alsace-Lorraine. Over the next few months, we made our way to the Rhine River. All the bridges were knocked out, and we made our crossing on pontoon bridges under heavy smoke screens. We crossed the Rhine near Mannheim, Germany, and our next crossing was the Neckar River at Heilbronn. It was now April 1945, and the days were getting longer and somewhat warmer.

One early afternoon, one of my crewmen started strumming on an old guitar, playing some old melodies. It was a nice spring day, and we were in a valley with a large hill in front of us. I had asked him to play some songs that I knew, and I started singing. I asked if he could play this melody entitled "Blue Moon." Here I was singing and entertaining all of the GIs in the field. Before I was able to complete the song, along came a jeep with a driver and an officer. They drove right up to us, and the officer stood in front of me and my guitar buddy and said, "Soldier, what the hell is wrong with you? Don't you know my infantry troops are on the other side of this hill right in front of your position, and the German troops are on the other side of our troop's position?" He told me how all his men had heard my singing, and he assured me that the Germans had probably heard it, too. He continued, "If my men get shelled or if your outfit gets shelled, you're going to be in trouble."

I apologized to the officer and said that I hadn't known that our battery was that close to his infantry unit. Basically, we were just to their rear. However, we were lucky. It turned out to be a very quiet evening. It's funny, but in war you often don't know where the front lines are.

By now the enemy was retreating rapidly. Our infantry had completely bypassed a few villages, and as our battalion entered the village of Baltmannsweiler, remnants of the Wehrmacht were surprised and gave up without resistance. We then found out there were more elements of the German army cutting us off to the rear. A skirmish followed; a few Jerries were killed and some surrendered. Others fled the area. We then patrolled the surrounding woods and captured approximately one hundred and fifty prisoners. Toward the end of April 1945, the war was winding down and the enemy was surrendering everywhere. It was on May 8, 1945, with a sigh of relief that the war ended in Europe. The war in the Pacific theater was still blazing. So where did we go from here? Before the Allies signed an armistice with the German army, the German high command asked if they could continue the war against the Russians as there was much hatred between the two nations. Naturally the U.S. government rejected this proposal. Soon after the war ended, General Patton quickly began to despise the Russian Communists and attempted to get the American forces to push them out of Europe. He was trying to provoke an international incident so as to start an act of aggression against the Soviet Union. He really did not like the Soviet Army and he definitely was ready to go to war against them. Patton stated, "If it should be necessary to fight the Russians, the sooner we do it the better." The U.S. government was somewhat worried that General Patton might do something that may get us involved in a war with Russia. General Patton was relieved of his command and promoted to a higher position in our government.

Now that the war was over for us, and because we had spent most of our combat days living and fighting in the open fields of Europe, we were all looking forward to settling down for a while. We dreamed of a nice small village where we could have a bed to sleep in, a bathtub to bathe in, and of course a roof over our heads. And, oh yes, some *ooh la la,* too!

On May 10, 1945, two days after the war in Europe ended, our battery was ordered to move. It was to a small village called Geradstetten. It was approximately eighteen miles east of Stuttgart. Our officers met with the bürgermeister (mayor) of the village and told him that we were going to occupy the schoolhouse and two civilian houses. The officers chose two houses and ordered the owners of these homes to vacate them within the hour. They had to leave everything except personal belongings. The neighbors invited the evicted owners to stay with them during this period that we occupied the homes. One of the homes was for the officers, and the other was used as a holding area for captured German soldiers.

All the GIs bunked at the school. We threw our belongings in the schoolhouse, and some of the guys found a soccer ball. Within a few minutes, we had formed sides and started to play a game. It was an exceptionally warm day, and after playing for an hour or so, we were perspiring heavily. One GI mentioned there was a small river in the valley, so my buddy Frank and I decided to walk there. It did look inviting, so we removed our clothing down to our shorts and jumped in the water.

A short while later, I looked up on the bank and saw two young women standing there. They were waving and smiling at us. *Ooh la la,* here we go again! Frank and I didn't waste any time getting out of the water and getting dressed. As we were approaching the young women, they told us that they were from Russia and that for the last few years they had been living in the wooden barracks by the water's edge. With sign language, we promised them that we would return at five o'clock, showing them the time on our watches. The young women agreed to meet us then. We found out that the two barracks were occupied by elderly men and women, girls, and children, but no young men. These young women said they were slave workers.

A little later that day, we heard that there was a distillery a few miles down the road. I jumped into a three-quarter-ton truck with a few guys. When we arrived, the German proprietor was a little frightened of us, but we were polite and asked if he would give us some liquor for some

American cigarettes? He obliged, and I believe we had a fair trade. Driving back to the village, we had to be very careful that the officers did not see us with the liquor. I drove the truck to the back of the school, and we put the liquor cases in the cellar via the back door.

A little before 5:00 p.m., Frank and I were getting ready to leave the schoolhouse for our "dates" when we found out the MPs were patrolling the village. We were not supposed to leave the schoolhouse, but, heck, that was not going to stop us. We had two Russian girls waiting for us. We went to the rear of the schoolhouse, only to discover all the doors were now locked. However, between the first and second floors was a large window. We opened it and found it was a six-foot drop to the ground. We dropped down and slowly made our way to the barracks where the girls were waiting. They were happy to see us and everything went just as we had planned.

A short time later, along came about four GIs running by us and telling Frank and me to hide, that the MPs had spotted them. We hid in some bushes near the water's edge, and the MPs didn't see either of us. They went right by and continued after the other guys. The only way for the GIs to escape was to jump in the river and swim to the other side. The river was approximately seventy-five yards wide at that point, so it was no problem for them to get across. That is what they did.

Frank and I stayed with the young women for a short period of time, then left to get back to the schoolhouse. We promised the girls we would see them again the following day.

When we got back to the schoolhouse, we got in through the window with the help of some of our buddies. Later that evening was our time to celebrate the war's end, and oh, how we celebrated! There I was, drinking the night away, celebrating the American victory over the Nazis. It's true I never drank when I first entered the army, but this was an occasion to celebrate and I certainly did.

The next morning the first sergeant and a second lieutenant came to get us up for formation outdoors. Forget about it. We were a bunch of sad sacks. The captain wanted to know where we got the booze, but he never found out, and we continued having our little parties until the very last bottle was gone.

Previously during our journey through France, whenever we entered a village, the townspeople would offer us different types of wine to thank us for their liberation. By war's end, most of us had already consumed enough wine or alcohol to make us veterans. Regardless of whether a GI had ever drank before, he sure did the night of the war's end.

Now at this time, the French Moroccans were occupying the city of nearby Stuttgart. Since the war had just ended, these soldiers were getting drunk and causing havoc. They were raping the women and shooting civilians for no reason. It got completely out of hand. The US command ordered them out of Stuttgart and told them to go into the French zone. However, they didn't comply. Therefore, we were given live ammunition and ordered to go and force these Moroccans to move to the French zone.

As we were getting ready to move to the town, the Moroccans changed their minds and thought better of staying. They headed out to Tubingen, which was toward the French zone.

The Love of My Life

A few days after Germany's surrender, the captain ordered the first sergeant to hand out sheets of paper to all the chiefs of gun sections and sergeants of other sections. On the paper, we were supposed to nominate the names of any GIs who deserved the Bronze Star. When the first sergeant gave me this form and explained the situation, I was totally shocked. If our officers did not see fit to award us the medal during combat, how could I nominate myself or the others after combat was over? I thought about all our boys who gave their lives for our country and how they had deserved this medal. Now the army was giving it to anyone who asked for it? That was not right.

I gave back the form to the first sergeant with no names on it. Of course I was the only one who did not put any names from my gun section on the form. I would have been proud to have received the Bronze Star, but not the way the army was giving it out. I still believe I did the right thing.

About a week or so after the war ended, all of the GIs in my outfit in Geradstetten knew I was having an affair with the Russian girl named Toni. At this time, some other GIs were also having affairs with other girls in the village. Some of the soldiers couldn't or wouldn't engage in conversation or flirtation. Knowing I was intimate with this girl from the Russian barracks by the river, a group of my friends one evening were drinking and looking for women. They decided to enter the barracks where Toni lived, seek her out, and try to have their way with her.

One of the GIs that was with them left to find me at the schoolhouse where we lived. He called for me to come to the Russian barracks. When I arrived there, I told all the men to get back to the schoolhouse. Toni was shaking and crying, but happy I arrived when I did. I consoled her and promised I would protect her from the other soldiers.

The following day when I went to visit Toni, she told me she was going to my captain and wanted to point out the GIs who had tried to rape her. I knew it could lead to harsh penalties for the GIs. For all I knew, she could have also included me.

That same afternoon, the captain called all the soldiers to stand in formation in front of the schoolhouse. Toni was standing next to the captain and started pointing out some of the GIs that she thought had been trying to rape her. The soldiers were informed as to why we were being called to attention. Of course, I knew some of my buddies were in trouble. Toni pointed out two GIs that she recognized from the night before. They came forward, and then the captain dismissed the rest of the soldiers. Thank goodness she didn't implicate me with the others.

The following day, the officers held a hearing about this incident, and truthfully nothing came of it, with no action taken by the army. Then I had second thoughts about Toni. Should I continue having a relationship with her? I decided to end it with Toni. It was a tough decision to make because she was a very warm and affectionate young woman. Within the next few months, all slave laborers and displaced persons in Germany were sent home to their native countries.

On May 15, 1945, they assigned me and three other soldiers to the second house that had been evacuated by the owners. The house was a holding area for the German soldiers, whom we were still rounding up. Whenever we confronted them, they would just surrender. We would hold them in this house until the MPs could take them to prison camps.

The next morning, along came two young women and their stepmother. They happened to be the owners of the house. They were the ones who were evicted by our officers and were now living next door with their neighbors. They were also ordered to come and clean up the mess we GIs made from day to day. We would take the glasses and plates from the kitchen cabinets and leave them in the sink after using them. The house was untidy because we never put anything back. The biggest problems the owners had were the scuff marks made by the bottoms of our combat boots on the wooden floors. They had to get on hands and knees with fine steel wool to get those off. So every morning for the remainder of our stay in Geradstetten, they would come and clean the floors, the kitchen, and the bedrooms.

Let me tell you something. The minute I saw the younger girl, I flipped. She was a natural beauty, about five foot seven inches tall and about a hundred and twenty pounds, with light brown hair and eyes. That morning when she, her stepmother, and her sister were preparing to clean the house, I approached her. I thought I wouldn't have any problems becoming acquainted with her, since I considered myself to be quite personable. I had never had any problems with women before.

Now let me tell you what happened next. I looked right at her and said, "Good morning, *fraulein*." I expected her to stop mopping the floor and look directly at me and give me a response. Forget about it. She kept on working and never looked at me once. She ignored me and my comment. I couldn't believe she wouldn't even look at me.

The next morning when she and her stepmother and her sister arrived, I approached her and said "Good morning, *fraulein*" again. She continued working and totally ignored me again. This went on for a few more days. She would not acknowledge me whatsoever. I could not believe it. I imagined that it was because we Americans threw them out of their house and made them come back in every day to clean up our mess. But on the fourth morning, again I said, "Good morning, *fraulein*," and all of a sudden she looked directly at me and said "*Guten morgen*." I felt thrilled that she finally acknowledged me. Truthfully, I wanted her to know that at this time I wanted to be her friend and then let nature take its course.

From then on, I saw her every morning and every afternoon when she sat behind her neighbors' house and read during her lunch. The army had issued the GIs a small English-German/German-English dictionary. One day as I saw her sitting there reading, I decided to approach her and asked if it would be okay for me to sit next to her. She agreed. She told me her name was Irene Baur and that she was going to be nineteen in a few weeks.

With this little book, I was able to converse and let her know I wanted to be her friend. I also let her know that I wanted to protect her from some of the GIs who were a little too aggressive toward her.

Irene as a youngster – 7 years old
Even then she looked pretty.

With every passing day, she was much more relaxed with me. We became good friends. On her nineteenth birthday, I was able to get some coffee and a cake from the mess kitchen. I invited a few of my friends to share in a party at her neighbors' house. She looked so happy and so pretty. It's strange, but I made no attempt to give her a kiss. To be honest, I didn't want to mess up my chances for the future.

By this time, she knew all about my parents, my brothers and sisters, and me, and about our move from the Bronx to Brooklyn. I would see Irene every morning, then again at noon when she was reading. That was it. The GIs were not allowed to fraternize with "the enemy." That's right. Irene was considered "the enemy" by the US Army. We were not even allowed to take walks together. It was against army regulations.

Irene told me that in April 1945, they had heard the American soldiers were not far from entering their village, Geradstetten. Most of the civilian population decided it was best to gather up their personal items and head up into the hills outside of the village, since there might be some shelling and possibly fighting with the Germans soldiers who would try to defend the village.

However, not all of the villagers decided to go to the bunkers in the hills. Irene, her sister Marianne, and Marianne's child Christa initially went to the bunkers, having decided it was best not to be in the village when the Americans came. After being at the bunkers all day and into the night, Irene heard one of her neighbors say that she thought the Americans had already gone through the village. So, by herself at 4:00 a.m., Irene decided it was safe to go back home.

There was a moon out that night and she could see pretty well. As she was approaching the town, walking in alleyways between the houses, suddenly she felt something sharp at her back and heard someone say, "Halt." When Irene left for the hills, she had put on dark clothing, black pants and jacket, and a kerchief on her head. The American soldier thought she was a boy, and they took her as a prisoner of the US Army. The soldier marched her to a home where other prisoners had been taken. They were surprised to find out she was a girl from the town; she was lucky no one shot at her. They said she should not have been out that time of night and then released her. When I asked her why she didn't wait 'til morning to come back, she said that she honestly believed the Americans had come through the village and gone on.

Irene on bridge, 1945

Irene's Family

Irene's father was born in 1893 and her mother in 1895. They married in 1919 and had three children: Marianne, born in 1921; Irene, born in 1926; and Heinz, born in 1929. Irene's father was a carpenter (licensed house builder). He worked with architects and built the entire frames and interior woodwork throughout new houses. In 1926, Irene's father built a two-family home that the Baur family occupied.

In 1932, when Irene's mother was thirty-seven years old, she died of kidney disease. That left Irene's father alone with three young children to raise. Irene had just turned six and was sent to live with relatives. Her uncle's sister-in-law, Emma, came to help with the other children, cook, and clean the house. Within three months, Irene's father and Emma were married, and Irene was sent back home to live again. Irene always told me that she never received love or caring from her stepmother, but she was treated well, and her stepmom was a good homemaker.

Her biological mother's family had lived in Geradstetten for many generations and had parcels of land for growing vegetables, fruit, and vineyards. This gave Irene many chores as a youngster, like keeping house, helping cook meals, and working in the different fields.

Irene's older sister, Marianna, was engaged to a German sergeant named Willy, and in 1943 they were married in Cologne's Catholic Cathedral. A year later, their daughter Christa was born. It was not until July 1944 that Willy received a furlough and came home to see his daughter for the first and, unfortunately, the last time. He returned to the front line in France and within a few months was killed. The entire family took Willy's death very hard.

During the war, when people were being bombed out of their homes in the cities, they were sent to small villages to live away from the bombs. People were looking for housing everywhere, and Irene's father was ordered by the bürgermeister to give the upstairs of their house to another couple and their child, which he did, as did most people in the villages. Irene's family had a few chickens and rabbits, as well as what vegetables they were able to grow in the back garden. Each morning the hens would gargle, and the GIs would run out to the henhouse and look for fresh-laid eggs for their breakfast. Irene's stepmother made sure Irene was ready to get there first to gather the eggs for their family. So it was a race each morning to see who would get to the henhouse first. Irene's stepmother was very happy when, on June 9, 1945, we were ordered to leave Geradstetten for a town called Schwäbisch Gmünd. This meant that we would be leaving their house and they could finally move back in again.

When the GIs arrived in Geradstetten in 1945, Christa was only sixteen months old. When she saw all the soldiers, she didn't understand, and it made her timid and shy. As time went on, when I would come to visit, Christa knew each time I came that I had gum or chocolates with me. She would come to me with her hands behind her back as soon as I arrived. Approaching me, she would extend her hands and hand me a bunch of dandelions that she had picked in the fields. She was so sweet and shy. I would accept the dandelions, and I could tell she was waiting for me to reward her with a chocolate bar or some gum. I would open my little carry bag and take out a stick of gum and a bar of chocolate to thank her for the flowers. I can still see the expression on her face when she got the gum and chocolate.

When Irene and I married, Christa was a flower girl at our wedding. Today she is sixty-eight years old and is as beautiful now as she was back then. In 1946 Irene's widowed sister Marianne met and married a German navy veteran and went on to have three more children: Heidi, Irene, and Thomas. Christa acquired three half siblings.

The town of Schwäbisch Gmünd was approximately fifteen miles east of Geradstetten, and I promised Irene I would be back to visit. Most GIs were free of duty from Saturday afternoon 'til Monday morning. She was such a sweet and good-natured girl; I knew I just had to come back to see Irene again.

Irene at 17 years of age

The following Sunday, I hitched a ride back to Geradstetten and she was delighted to see me. We were able to take a walk together for the first time. I have to admit it was quite romantic. In fact, I was starting to fall in love with her. I am sure Irene was also happy when we were together. It felt great just being with her. I couldn't wait for Saturday afternoons when we GIs were free for the weekend.

Irene then invited me to come back the following Sunday to have dinner with her and her family. I was really happy about that and accepted the invitation. It would be the first time I would have a real German meal. When I arrived at her house, Irene was at the front door, and it felt good seeing and being able to be with her again. The meal consisted of meat (I had no idea what kind it was), spatzle (a noodle that looks like spaghetti), and, of course, potato salad. They were hoping I would enjoy this meal, and truthfully, it wasn't bad, considering I never had that kind of food before.

Well, one day approximately six months later, Irene asked me if I knew what kind of meat I had had on that first Sunday. I confessed I had no idea, and I was not sure I wanted to know. I found out it was rabbit meat. That was the only meat they had around at the time. She didn't want to tell me, not being sure how an American felt about eating rabbit.

At the end of June 1945, we shipped out to a town called Herrenberg. This was about fifteen miles southwest of Stuttgart. The One Hundredth Infantry Division made Stuttgart our division headquarters. All of the division's troops were stationed within a twenty-mile radius.

Around 10:00 p.m. one Sunday night, after my usual visit with Irene, I was leaving to return to my base in Herrenberg. It was about two months after the war had ended. I was able to hitch a ride to Stuttgart, but I still had a long way to go. I started walking, hoping to catch a jeep or truck ride back.

No vehicle came along at all. It got to be approximately 2:00 a.m. and I was still walking along the road when suddenly I heard a vehicle coming my way. As it approached, I waved it down. It was an old German truck. I asked if they could take me to Herrenberg, and the driver said he could take me to a town just before that town. I told him it was good, that I could walk the rest of the way after he dropped me off.

***Lou and Irene in Germany,
shortly after the war ended
in Europe, May 1945***

I went around to the back of the truck and jumped in. There were about ten men sitting there, and when I looked closely at them, they were all German soldiers who had just been released from a prisoner of war camp and were on their way home. I said to myself, "Lou, you are in trouble now." Irene had taught me some German to get by with, but here I was sitting with ten German soldiers at two o'clock in the morning with not another soul in sight.

The first thing I did was to start a conversation with them. I told them I was from Brooklyn and asked if any of them had relatives in America. I was trying to make them feel more relaxed with me. Some of them understood some of what I said. Most of these men were happy to be on their way home and were very quiet. No question, I was quite nervous sitting with them, but I tried to make them believe I was a friend and not an enemy. Truthfully, I couldn't wait for the truck driver to stop and tell me this was where he turned off so that I could get off and walk the rest of the way to Herrenberg.

About fifteen minutes later, he did just that, and I was quite relieved to depart the truck. I really never felt any resentment toward the German soldiers, but under those circumstances, I didn't know how they would react toward me. I hopped off the truck, said goodbye to the soldiers, and gave the driver some cigarettes. Then I continued walking until I got back to base.

A few months after the war ended in Europe, the army issued color posters to all units in Germany with photos of the medals and ribbons the GIs won during the war, exact in size and color. We found a woman in town who could sew and showed her the photos, then told her which ribbons or medals we had been awarded. She would then copy them onto our army Eisenhower dress jacket. This dress jacket was originally worn by General Dwight D. Eisenhower, and later it became the standard dress jacket for the entire army. We would wear this jacket at special events, during parades, retreat, when on leave, or off the base. We all looked pretty sharp in them. The seamstress had every color thread, and would sew every ribbon stitch by stitch, color by color. When she was done, sure enough, they looked perfect. It was hard to tell they were not real ribbons.

Goodbye to My Buddy

At that time, just after the end of the war, there were many displaced persons (DPs). They included Polish, Russian, and other nationalities. Eventually they would be sent back to their native lands, but that didn't happen for another three or four months. The US Army distributed olive drab uniforms to all the males in the DP camps, and this made them look very much like American soldiers. The DPs then took it upon themselves to run rampant, assaulting and robbing the German people. The Germans thought American soldiers were attacking them. So the army took away the uniforms, had them dyed a dark blue, and returned them to the DPs. Now the German people could tell the difference between the Americans and the DPs, and the assaults and robberies soon stopped.

Not far from Herrenberg was a Polish DP camp. Most American army units would take a few of the DPs to work with the mess sergeant. That made things easier on the GIs. Our outfit took on three Polish DPs. They worked in our kitchen and relieved our soldiers of that duty.

One day when the DPs were off duty, they wanted to go to this camp and visit with their countrymen. The problem was they had no transportation. They approached my buddy Frank and asked if he could help them. Frank volunteered to give them a ride. They all jumped into a jeep and away they went. I didn't know Frank had taken these guys to the camp. There they drank and danced and as usual had a good time.

After being there all day and evening, they left to come back to our base. I later heard that Frank somehow or another left the road while driving the jeep, and he and two of the three displaced Polish workers were killed. Very early the next morning, I was notified that Frank was laid out in a garage in town with an MP standing guard. I quickly ran to this garage and told the MP who I was and that I wanted to see my friend. He agreed to let me in.

Inside, there he was, my best friend. I thought of the many things we had gone through and the times we had had together. I looked at him lying there with a head wound and kept saying, "Why, Frank? Why?" We had often talked about how we would visit each other in the States and stay in touch with each other. Now it was all over; all our plans were for naught. I tilted my head to get a better look at his face and once more said, "Why?"

When I left the garage, I thanked the MP. He asked if Frank was a close friend. I answered, "No, he was more like a brother."

That evening I was depressed, as were some of the other GIs who had known Frank. We talked about all the good times we had had together. Many times we had gone on three-day passes during training in the States. Frank was an excellent dancer, and he and I went to the service club when they held dances. We did many things together. Yes, he was liked by everyone. The GIs and I did some drinking that evening, and I just cried.

I was miserable, and I longed to be with Irene. She knew how close I was to Frank, and she also knew him well. The next morning, I went to the edge of town and hitched a ride into Geradstetten. I told Irene about Frank and we both cried for him. It was a sad time for both of us.

That same day I went back to base and was told I was AWOL. This means "absent without official leave."

Lou lowering the American flag
at retreat formation in Summer 1945
Herrenberg, Germany

The Charges

As a result of the AWOL, I got a summary court martial. At that time, I was a corporal, and they busted me down to private and gave me hard labor and forfeit of pay for one month. After that, I was back to pulling guard duty and work detail.

My biggest problem was I was not able to see Irene, since her mom would not let her come to visit me. There was only one way to see her: take the chance and try not to get caught. In July, after pulling three out of four shifts of guard duty, I asked one of my buddies if he would take over my last shift of two hours for me. He agreed and I was headed for Geradstetten to see my Irene.

Unfortunately, my commanding officer somehow found out, and when I returned to base, they got me again. It was, "Here we go again, Lou, another court martial."

In those days, there were three levels of court martial. A summary court martial had a penalty of up to a thirty days' fine (loss of wages) and hard labor. A special court martial could get you imprisonment, a fine, and hard labor for six months. A general court martial was whatever the army wanted it to be, no limit of punishment. I was up for the special court martial. The court consisted of five officers to hear the case against me. My defense counsel was a young second lieutenant who didn't know the first thing about how to conduct himself in a court martial. The prosecution had a captain who was determined to win his case no matter what.

The charge of not being at my post and going AWOL for twenty-four hours was baloney. My buddies had filled in for me for two hours. During the trial, all the boys from my battery testified in my defense. Every word was taken down by the court's stenographer. Basically, the prosecution had no case, but from what I was hearing, they wanted to put me in prison for the maximum time of six months.

When the case rested, the jury of five officers went to an adjoining room to vote on my sentence. While my lawyer and I waited in the courtroom, I noticed the jury foreman leaving the building. He couldn't do that. He was not supposed to leave the jury room before the verdict had been rendered. I told my counsel, but because he was a second lieutenant, he didn't dare say anything.

I believe the jury foreman left the courthouse to inform the colonel that they didn't have much of case to warrant a "six six six" verdict. Of course, I couldn't swear that is what happened. I assume the colonel was notified in advance, and I still believe he told the jury foreman to give me the maximum penalty. Yeah, Lou, and you got it!

When everyone was back in the courtroom, the five jury officers were seated side by side in front of a row of tables. I was told, "Private Candela, come forward. This jury hereby sentences you to six months in prison, six months' forfeit of pay, and six months of hard labor." My buddies couldn't believe it, but that's how the army works.

Then, while standing at attention before the jury, my lawyer said to me, "Private Candela, salute the members of the jury." There was no way was I going to salute these officers. According to army protocol, once a soldier is court-martialed and must serve time in an army prison, he no longer is in good standing as a soldier, and he no longer has the right to salute any officer.

I was still depressed about Frank's death. It didn't make any difference to the army. I knew before I went that there was a possibility of a court martial. How did it feel? Not good at all. But I somehow accepted what the army dished out to me.

Before two MPs took me away to a German Panzer camp that the Americans now occupied, I told a few buddies to get in touch with the IG, or Inspector General, in Stuttgart and to also let Irene know the situation. The IG reviews any reported injustice toward army personnel.

When I arrived at the fort, they had many prison cells, and I had the honor of occupying one of them. There was no cot to sleep on, and I asked the MPs, "Where's my bed?"

They both laughed and said, "The floor."

I answered, "The least you can do is give me a few blankets."

That much, they did. The following morning after chow, they took me out on work detail. At the end of the day, back in my cell, I discovered that the MPs had rummaged through my belongings and stole—yes, stole—my money and personal items. So much for our military police. Oh, yes, and they did give me a cot on the second day.

Meanwhile, back at my unit, my first sergeant told the captain that Candela had been railroaded, and that he and the other GIs from the outfit were going to the IG in Stuttgart to complain. My captain went berserk and said it was mutiny, and he would court martial the entire battery if they went. However, my captain then got in touch with the colonel, and guess what?

That's right. After ten days in prison, two MPs came, unlocked my cell door, and told me that they had orders to release me and take me back to my outfit. If it were not for my buddies going to bat for me, I would have served six months of hard labor in prison. That was the last time I was ever court-martialed.

Now I was hoping that the US government would allow GIs to marry German girls. Americans were marrying Japanese women, Italian women, every women on earth except German women. Why?

The war was still going on in the Pacific, and at the end of July 1945 we received orders that we were going back to the United States for thirty days and then going on to board troop ships in California. We would eventually end up invading the Japanese mainland. We would be leaving Germany shortly for Le Havre, France to get a ship back to the United States.

I went to see Irene to explain to her the news of our leaving for the Pacific. I asked her, if and when I get back home to Brooklyn after the war, if she would come to America. She said that she'd be too frightened to come alone, not knowing if I'd be there for her. But she promised she would wait, and if I still loved her, I would somehow come back to Germany for her. I promised the same.

Then on August 6, 1945, while we were preparing to leave Germany, the United States dropped the first atomic bomb on Hiroshima, Japan. Three days later, we dropped the second bomb, this time on Nagasaki. Our outfit was now in a holding position in Germany.

On August 14, Japan surrendered to the Allied Forces. We did not have to go to the Pacific. Now what did the future hold for Irene and me?

At that point there were a lot of GIs who had enough points for repatriation to the States and discharge. The points system consisted of so many points for each month of service and so many for each overseas duty. The guys with the most points got priority for discharge. All of the old-timers went home first. By October 1945, there were only a handful of our boys left from the original battery.

Near the end of November 1945, it was my time to go home and be discharged. I thought by this time the government would have lifted the ban on GIs marrying German women, but it hadn't yet.

I remember Eleanor Roosevelt visited Germany during this period. In one of her speeches, she spoke of all the GIs who wanted to marry German girls. She said that they were just homesick, and they should all go home and think about it. She didn't have any idea of what she was talking about, and I don't think Mrs. Roosevelt understood our feelings about this. If I had truly been homesick, I would have just gone home. Nevertheless, the government still kept the ban on marrying Germans and bringing them to the United States.

I just could not understand why the US government would not let the US soldiers marry their *frauleins*. What was the real reason for the ban? I thought it was unfair, especially after I had served my country proudly. My mom and pop knew all about my meeting Irene in May 1945, and that I wanted to marry her. Pop was happy for me, but Mom was really disappointed and thought it was Irene's fault that I was getting into trouble. Yep, poor Irene. She got on the wrong side of Mom from the very beginning. I was even thinking of signing up for another stretch in the army to be able to stay with Irene.

One day while reading *Stars and Stripes*, I saw an article that stated if a GI was due for discharge and wanted to sign up again, he had the option of signing up for six more months or for three years. I jumped at the opportunity and enlisted for the six months' duration.

Irene, Autumn 1945
Geradstetten, Germany

Lou, Autumn 1945, Geradstetten, Germany

On Christmas Day, 1945, Irene and I became engaged. Germany was still in ruins from the war and food was quite scarce. People bartered for goods. Irene's stepmother gave two chickens away in exchange for two gold rings. I asked Irene if she was sure she wanted to marry me, that I did not have a profession, I did not have a job waiting for me at home, and I did not even have a foreseeable future. I did say, though, that "As long as I have these two hands (which I held out to her), we are going to make it and be okay." Irene said that she didn't care what I had or didn't have, and promised she would always stay by me.

We were at Irene's house on this Christmas Day. Irene and I were extremely happy, and yet I felt that here I am, asking Irene to marry me, knowing I could never give her the things that she already had at her home in Germany. I did not have much to offer Irene. I definitely made her understand that there wasn't going to be a rosy picture for us if and when we went back home to America. Believe me, Irene was just a nineteen-year-old girl who was always happy when we were together.

While stationed in Ulm in January 1946, two other GIs and I received orders to report to a German prison that held many political prisoners. These men were civilians who were involved in war crimes against the Allied Forces. I had no idea what type of crimes they committed. I only knew that the US Army Intelligence Agency rounded them up after the war, interrogated them, and arrested them. Then they were tried for their crimes and sent to prison. Our orders were to transport twenty-four sick men to a prison hospital at another location in Germany. The army divided the prisoners into two groups. Three of us took twelve men in one truck, and another three GIs took the other twelve men in a second truck. The weather was very cold and there was lots of snow on the ground. The prisoners we were transporting were all middle-aged or elderly men. We GIs received quite a few boxes of K-rations for this long trip, but the prisoners did not receive any blankets or food for themselves.

Because of the bad weather, we soon lost the second truck, and our driver was not sure how to find the prison hospital. I was up front with the driver, and the other two GIs in our group were in the back with the ill men. It was a long, slow-moving drive, and at one point I told the driver to pull over. I asked the GIs if they would mind giving up some of their K-rations for the prisoners. The GIs agreed. The prisoners thanked us, and after eating, they couldn't wait for a cigarette. I think there were three cigarettes in each box. They thanked us again for everything.

Our driver still was not sure of his way to the hospital, and even though we were traveling slowly, the truck skidded off the road and into a ditch. We were lucky we did not flip over. I went to the main road and waited for an American vehicle to come by. Within a few minutes, an American jeep stopped and I told the GI driver what had happened. I asked him if his company was nearby and if he would get some help to get us out of the ditch. He said his outfit was stationed in the next village, and he would get someone to get us back up on the main road.

They came back in about fifteen minutes with a big truck that pulled us up and out of the ditch. I asked the sergeant if we could stop at his base and get the prisoners some hot food and a warm up. He said okay, and so we followed him back to his base. When we got there, I asked his first sergeant if the men could get some hot soup and bread; seeing they were sick, elderly men, the first sergeant said okay, but they had to stay in the truck. He did not want these prisoners in the mess hall. I asked if we could build a bonfire for the men to sit around and get warm while having their soup. Again, he said okay to that and helped us build the bonfire outside. When the prisoners were finished eating, we helped them back into the truck. I thanked all the GIs at this base for being so kind and helpful.

We started on our way again to the prison hospital. We still had a few hours to go, but the men were more comfortable for the rest of their journey. When we finally pulled into the hospital, it was about 8:00 p.m. Before I could get out of the truck, along came two MPs. They started to give me hell for not arriving hours ago. It seems that the first truck had arrived long before, and they had been waiting for us to show up. I told them about the truck going off the road and how we were lucky to get help from another company. I walked to the back and put down the tailgate to help the prisoners out. The MPs did not like this and ordered me to let the men disembark by themselves. Some of these men were not able to do so and needed help. I again started to assist them, and the MPs ordered me for a second time to stop and get away from the men, or they would arrest me.

The prisoners all managed to get off the truck, and many of them came up to me. They hugged me and thanked me for being so kind to them. Some of them were even crying. How in the world could those MPs just stand there and not care at all about helping their fellow man. I can't believe some people are so heartless. When all the prisoners were safely in the hospital, I felt a lot better, and we left.

On our way back, I thought about this very long, exhausting day and night, but I knew that those men were safe in a warm bed, and the next day our army doctors would help them get well again. You may ask why I did what I did. I always believed that it was right to help other human beings, people who through no fault of their own couldn't help themselves, whether it was because they were ill, handicapped, or had some other physical or mental problem. Some might say I only felt sorry for these Germans because I had a German girlfriend. That's BS.

By the spring of 1946, most of the GIs were gone and I kept getting transferred. I had one good thing going for me. Being a veteran, I did receive a bit of respect from all the officers and recruits who arrived in Germany in 1946. While stationed in Ludwigsberg, my captain asked if I would volunteer to give the recruits close-order drills and calisthenics in the morning. No problem. I enjoyed the privilege of giving those recruits a good workout each morning.

Irene and Lou, Springtime 1946
Ludwigsburg, Germany

In March 1946, my captain again called me into his office. He said he had good news for me. They were looking for spit and polish soldiers to be honor guards for all the diplomats and dignitaries who arrived at Templehof Airport in Berlin. He said he would put me in for sergeant immediately if I agreed to volunteer. I thanked him for his trust in me, but if I had gone to Berlin, Irene and I could not see each other again. Berlin was divided into four zones: American, English, French, and Russian. If a GI tried to go into the American occupation zone in Germany, he had to travel through the Russian zone. There, he might have been stopped and arrested. At that time after the war, the Americans and the Russians were not getting along at all. I explained to my captain that I had a German girlfriend and that I was able to see her quite often. I was quite content with that. However, I again thanked him for his thoughtfulness.

By May 1946, the war had been over for almost a year, my six months' reenlistment was almost over, and the government still refused to let me marry Irene. What was I going to do now? Reenlist again. It had to be three years this time, but I had no other choice. I was getting tired of army life, but it was the only thing I could see to do.

Then, a few days before I was to reenlist again, I read an article in *Stars and Stripes* looking for GIs who were due for discharge to sign up as civilians and work for the War Department. *There you go again, Lou; you certainly are a lucky guy.*

I did get discharged in Heidelberg on May 24, 1946 and went to Frankfurt, where I received employment as a civilian working in the town of Oberesslingen. Lucky me, it was not far from Irene's village. The department I worked for was called the CCD, or Civil Censorship Division. It was a government agency whose main purpose was to intercept telephone calls, open and read all mail, and generally control any communication among the German population. The object was to hunt down any Nazi war criminals who were wanted by the Allied authorities.

Our department employed Allied personnel who wrote and spoke not only English, but German also. These included nationals from countries like Denmark, England, the United States, and a few other places. My position was supervisor of security for the entire compound, including the homes that these civilian employees occupied. I and five other ex-GIs held the same supervisory position. Then we had one person in charge of our overall department.

It was nice being a civilian again and having my own apartment. When not on duty, I was able to wear my civilian clothes that I had asked my mom to ship over to me. Everything fit me well, and I looked sharp in my old zoot suit. For all you young Turks who don't know what a zoot suit was, let me explain. It was a single-breasted suit with a jacket long enough to reach the bottom of my thumbs and baggy pants. The pant legs tapered from the knee to the ankle at sixteen inches. The belt line was above my hips. If you have ever seen the movies of Cab Callaway, a band leader in the Thirties and Forties, then you've seen the zoot suit, although the cut of their suits was extreme. Regardless, Callaway looked good when he sang "Minnie the Moocher" (hidey hidey hidey hi).

We had a great setup there for all the employees. We had our own mess hall with menus at every meal. We had our own private nightclub with a German orchestra every night and dancing and drinking. But there was one thing missing for me: my Irene. I must say there were many young girls from Denmark and England who were very pretty. I did take notice. I always had an eye for a pretty woman. One of our boys married a beautiful Danish girl, and they made a very lovely couple.

In the summer of 1946, I went to Geradstetten and asked Irene's stepmother if she would give her permission to let Irene come and visit me in Oberesslingen. Finally, she gave in and gave us permission, and I was able to take Irene to where I was living. We went to the nightclub in the evening, and since she did not know how to dance, I taught her some steps. Irene never learned to speak any English while we were in Germany. We only spoke German to each other since she taught me the language. By living there, I was also able to pick up words and phrases and speak with the locals. After that, Irene's stepmom let her visit with me from time to time, and it was an adventure for Irene.

Usually when I visited Irene's family, I took candy with me for the children who would gather around the jeep; I would gladly give them any goodies I had. So in December 1946, I went to the PX, or post exchange in Heidelberg, something like a general store for the Americans and Allied personnel. I went to the candy counter and bought as much candy, chocolates, gum, and goodies as I could fit in a travel bag. Truthfully, I can't recall how much it cost me to buy all that, but whatever the price was, it was worth it. Those children had never had much candy or gum until the GIs arrived in Germany.

As I approached Geradstetten, I stopped at the schoolhouse. As usual when the children saw me coming, they surrounded the jeep looking for some goodies. I opened the travel bag and started giving out the candy and gum. Then I continued on to Irene's house to give her the rest of the candy. As I arrived there, a small group of children formed around the jeep. Within a few minutes, more children kept coming. Then Irene came out of her home to help me hand out the goodies for the children to enjoy. We had a little candy left over for us, and Irene was happy we did this for the village children. I felt just like Santa Claus and was happy that I had bought all the stuff at the PX.

On another occasion when I visited the PX in Heidelberg to buy some clothing, I noticed a group of GIs gathered under a large platform. As I approached the area to see what was going on, I saw a soldier at the platform auctioning off odds and ends. I stood in the audience for a while and was not really interested. As I was getting ready to leave, the soldier called to the GIs and said he had something to auction that he knew everyone there would be thrilled to give to their lover. Believe it or not, it was a brand-new pair of women's nylon stockings. Now I became interested. When I first met Irene and used to go see her on Sundays, she would get all dressed up but wear long brown stockings. They just didn't look right. Now, here was my chance to get her a pair of real nylon stockings.

The bidding began: the first bid was five dollars. I decided to bid and keep on bidding. The problem was that every GI there was bidding on the stockings for the same reason as I was, for their girlfriend or lover.

The bidding got over thirty dollars, but I kept on bidding because I wanted to see how beautiful Irene looked in those stockings. Finally, when I bid thirty-five dollars, that was the last bid, and I received the much-deserved prize for Irene. Many of the GI's there congratulated me and said that whoever I was going to give them to must be worthy of them for me to spend all that money. I really must be in love with her.

The next time I visited Irene, I handed her the gift and she was surprised and thrilled to get them. The following Sunday, she was waiting for me to come and was all dressed up, wearing those nylon-for-the-war-effort nylons. (Nylons were scarce in those days because the army used it for tents and parachutes.) I said to her, "Now you look like an American girl."

What troubled me was that after the war ended, the US Army Intelligence Agency rounded up as many Nazi rocket scientists as they could to work for the United States on rockets that would go into space. Now hear this: these were the same Nazi scientists who had worked under Hitler's command. They were firing V-1 and V-2 rockets into England, causing fatalities and fires and destroying buildings where the rockets hit. The US government set these men and their families up with all the comforts in America as long as they worked on the rocket programs.

It was certainly a smart move for the United States to bring German scientists to America because it was Dr. Wernher von Braun and his team of associates who helped the United States with our space program. I applaud the United States' action, but there is one thing I can't understand. Irene was not a Nazi and she was no threat to anyone, either in Germany or in America. So why in the world did they deny me the right to marry Irene and bring her home with me? I honestly would like to know the real reason for this.

Finally, almost two years after the war ended, the US government gave Americans the authorization to marry their *frauleins*. Irene and I applied for a marriage license. We filled out what seemed to be a hundred forms. Next, the US Army Intelligence Agency investigated Irene's past.

She had been thirteen when the war started and nineteen when it ended. They wanted to know if she had any ties to Nazi organizations: was she a Nazi or a war criminal? After two months of investigation, the US government finally gave us permission to marry. There was one stipulation: we both had to leave Germany within two months of the marriage. I said to myself, "You know, Lou, I think it's time we went home."

Now we had to plan our wedding. After the war ended, German currency couldn't buy you anything, but American cigarettes were worth more than gold. All bartering in Germany was strictly with American cigarettes. No money changed hands, just cigarettes. That's how everyone managed to get by. For our wedding plans, we needed what every wedding reception would need: food, liquor, and a wedding cake. With the help of the mess chef, who promised to make the cake, all I had to do was get the eggs. No problem there: I gave the chicken farmer cigarettes for the eggs. The liquor was exchanged for American cigarettes; same for the photographer. I worked with a Danish couple, and they offered to drive Irene, her brother-in-law, and me to a pig farm in Bavaria. There, for the main course, we exchanged cigarettes for a nice, rosy, fat pig.

You must be asking yourself where I got all these cigarettes. In Oberesslingen where I was working, there were many GIs stationed in town. I would approach the soldiers and buy cigarettes from them for thirty-five dollars a carton in American currency. I have no idea how many cigarettes I bought, but I needed all of them for the salads, vegetables, bread, flowers, and entertainment. Our commanding officer at CCD willingly allowed me the honor of using the nightclub for the big event.

Next, I went to the American Catholic chaplain. I asked if he would perform the ceremony. He said he would be happy to do so. "And by the way, is your girlfriend a Catholic?"

I answered, "No, but it shouldn't matter."

Like hell it shouldn't matter, at least as far as the priest was concerned. He went on and on about how he couldn't marry us unless

Irene was a Catholic. He sounded like my old captain rather than a chaplain. His attitude wasn't unusual, though. Back in the 1920s, 30s, and 40s, if you wanted to marry in a Catholic church, it was standard procedure that both parties had to be Catholic. Most Catholic priests at that time wouldn't marry two people unless they were both Catholic. They wanted to make sure that the children would be brought up as Catholics. And there I was asking this Catholic army chaplain to marry Irene and me. How many more obstacles would we have to overcome just to get married? It seemed like it never ended.

I then had to go see Irene and let her know what the chaplain had said about not being able to marry us unless she was a Catholic. She cried but realized she had no choice but to go along with it and convert.

Soon after the war ended, most people of German descent living in Europe were ordered to return to Germany. It might have been fate or just a very strange coincidence, but one of these people was a Catholic priest. He had set up his church in a small factory in the village of Grunbach, which was next to Irene's village of Geradstetten. Irene and I went to this village and met with the priest, Father John. We asked him if he would convert her to Catholicism. He said he would, and Irene started classes for six weeks. He baptized her and she received her First Holy Communion. We asked Father if he would also perform our wedding ceremony, and he was delighted to do so.

Our Big Day Arrives

On the morning of our wedding, Saturday, June 7, 1947, my best man had arranged with the Catholic Church of St. Paul's in Oberesslingen for a special mass for Irene and me, at 7:00 a.m. I had many wonderful friends, and they all helped in some way to make this a wedding that no one would ever forget. After the church, we went to the photo studio for pictures. Then we drove to Geradstetten.

My coworkers had arranged for a few taxis and two buses to take Irene's relatives and friends, including the village soccer team and, of course, Father John, to the church in Oberesslingen for the wedding ceremony at 3:00 p.m. We were running a little late, about one hour, but everything went smoothly. It was a good thing I understood German. Father John only spoke German, and of course the entire ceremony was in German.

Irene's aunt had some white satin material that she had obtained prior to the war, and another aunt was a seamstress. Together they made a lovely dress for Irene. She borrowed shoes and a bridal veil. There were flowers awaiting us at the church, and we also picked up some more flowers before we left Oberesslingen. Then I married my Irene.

After the ceremony, we were all assembled at our tables in the nightclub. We picked up our champagne glasses, and I had the honor of toasting my bride and my good fortune. I remember saying how happy I was, how thankful, and how extremely lucky to have met and married a wonderful young woman like Irene. I also thanked everyone present who supported our wedding. My German was only fair, so I made it short, but the wedding party still laughed at my accent. At the end of my short speech, I lifted my glass high and said, "*Prosit!*" The word means cheers or good luck or, as we in America would say, "Here's to you!"

The wedding reception was just beautiful. We had Irene's parents sitting next to her and Father John sitting next to me. Prior to the wedding, I was able to speak to the orchestra leader. I wanted the first song that Irene and I were going to dance to be "Let Me Call You Sweetheart." That would be our first song and would always be a special song for us. It was a little difficult for Irene because she did not dance too well, but I will never forget that dance. The entire evening went perfectly. The food, drinks, wedding cake, music, and dancing—all of them were perfect. We even had a private entertainment group. Those memories will be with us to stay for the rest of our lives.

City Hall in Oberesslingen, Germany
where we were officially married
June 7, 1947

Our Wedding Day, June 7, 1947
Oberesslingen, Germany

Lou and Irene cutting our wedding cake

Mr. & Mrs. Louis Candela
Two really happy people!

For our honeymoon, I made arrangements to stay at Garmisch in the Bavarian Alps. The US government and the US Army had taken over the entire area and used it as a rest and recreation center for all Americans. Halfway up the Alps was a very large lake called Lake Eibsee. A hotel overlooked the lake, and they gave us a beautiful, lake-view room. At night, we would take a cable car down to the village. The nightclub was beautifully decorated and the music there was great. Night after night they played this one song that was popular with all the GIs in Europe. It was written about a girl who would stand by the barracks' gate waiting for her lover. The title was "Lili Marlene." This German song was so popular that you heard it wherever you went, even in the United States. After waiting for so long to be married, our honeymoon at Garmisch was like a dream come true. Now we were finally at the beginning of our future together.

A few days before leaving Geradstetten for Bremerhaven to board the transport to New York, Irene's brother Heinz and I were fooling around with a soccer ball, kicking it back and forth. I had on only moccasins, and when I kicked the ball one time, my foot slipped halfway out of the shoe. As I landed on the ground, I twisted my ankle. It hurt for a while, but I didn't think anything of it.

In early July, on the morning we left Geradstetten for Bremerhaven, Irene's family, friends, and relatives accompanied us to the local train station for our last goodbyes. There were many hugs and kisses, but most of all a lot of crying. Can you imagine Irene saying goodbye to all her family, not knowing if she would ever see any of them again? Thinking back on it, she took a big gamble leaving everything behind to go to America with a guy who had nothing to offer her except a determination to make her happy. As the train left Geradstetten, Irene and I waved our goodbyes to her folks. She cried and was sad.

When we arrived at Stuttgart, we had to change trains to Frankfurt, then onto Bremerhaven. Arriving in Bremerhaven, we were assigned a room in a building that looked like a hotel. There were many such buildings, all looking alike. We were to be there for at least a week before embarking for the United States.

During this time, my ankle was swelling up and I couldn't walk too well. I went to the administration office, and the man there directed me to the army hospital at the Bremerhaven base. The technician took an X-ray, and sure enough, the ankle had a fracture. They put me in a cast from the foot to just below my knee. It had a ball at the base so I was able to walk on the leg.

As we boarded the transport, I thought Irene and I were going to share a room together, but forget about it. They put her in a very large room with other ladies. I got stuck way down at the bottom end of the ship near the propeller. It was dark, greasy, and smelly. When the rear of the ship rose and the propeller came even partially out of the water, the whole back of the ship would vibrate. I honestly thought the ship was coming apart. It was somewhat scary, but in time I got used to it.

There we were, newlyweds, and we were separated for the entire journey. In the mornings, I would meet Irene for breakfast and we would go for a walk, but only in designated areas. The ship had many off-limits sections. We would also meet for lunch and dinner. Somehow, I accepted it, since I knew we were going home to Brooklyn to start our new life together.

During the crossing, we encountered some rough weather and Irene did not feel too well. I asked the navy personnel in the galley if they had something I could give her to feel better. They gave me lemon slices. It helped her a lot and she never did get sick.

I remembered the first time when I was in the army and on the ship going to France. Our battery was assigned to the galley to serve the other GIs their meals. We had many days of rough seas, and I, too, was feeling a little queasy. The navy personnel in the galley gave me dried biscuits to help keep me from getting seasick. That worked pretty well, too. I was assigned to serve food to the soldiers, and as they went along the line to the next server and so on, some of the boys couldn't help but heave. What a mess. If they tried eating again, they just got sick, so as time went on, fewer and fewer GIs came to the dining room.

I remembered another incident while on our way to France. Whenever we GIs were ordered to take showers, we had to travel down a long corridor first. The MPs told all the enlisted men to walk down the left-hand side of the corridor, single file. The officers walked down the right-hand side. I did not realize it then, but we enlisted men were taking saltwater showers. The officers were taking freshwater showers. I thought to myself, "This is not fair."

The next time we showered, I got in the line with the officers and got my freshwater shower. Of course, there were two MPs standing at the shower doors, but I had no problem getting past them. Every time we showered, I always did this. You must be wondering how did I do this without being detected as an enlisted man. Simple, Dr. Watson. We were all naked going down the corridor. The MPs had no way of knowing who was enlisted or an officer. I must confess that a fresh water shower felt really good.

As for our journey to New York, overall, we had quite a few days of rough seas and they forbade us to go out on deck. Approximately three quarters of the way there, the ship's captain received an SOS call from a freighter that a sailor on board needed an appendix operation. It took us a day off course to meet the freighter. As the two ships were side by side, a line was thrown to the freighter. They secured the sick sailor on a gurney and slid him on the line to our ship. The doctors on board our ship operated on the sailor, and as far as I know he remained on our ship to New York. It took us one more day to get back on course, so instead of reaching New York in ten days, we arrived two days late. We were now going to arrive in Staten Island on Saturday evening. A few days prior to arriving, I entered the communications room and got permission to call my mom and tell her when and where we were to arrive.

We pulled into port on Saturday night, but we had to wait until Sunday morning for the pilot to board the ship and for the tugboats to guide us to port. On August 2, 1947, my wife and I finally arrived in Stapleton, Staten Island, New York, USA. My mom was so excited, she told all the relatives when we would dock, and sure enough, when I looked out the porthole I saw Mom, Pop, brothers Frank and Mike, Grandma, and two of my uncles. I waved to them from the porthole. I was very excited to see them all, and I could not wait to get off the ship. Finally, Irene and I were back home.

The army unloaded the army personnel and their families first, then the dignitaries, and so on down the line. Irene and I were about the last ones to leave the ship. I guess they went by priority, and Irene and I were not priority people. By the time we disembarked, my relatives had been waiting many hours and were getting tired and depressed that we hadn't come off the ship yet. Then, finally, there were Irene and Lou.

Home at Last

What a great feeling it was to greet my folks again. It had been almost three years since I left for France. Lots of hugs and kisses all around. My mom looked at Irene from all angles. She was trying to figure why her son would get into so much trouble over this girl. Right from the beginning, my mom didn't like Irene.

It was arranged that we were to stay at my parents' house in Bay Ridge, Brooklyn until my cast came off and I could look for a job and save a few bucks. We planned to move out to our own apartment as soon as we could. Mom had a small house with three bedrooms. My brothers Mike and Frank were still single and now had to share the second bedroom, while Irene and I were in the third.

After a few days, Irene and I went shopping for clothes. I had approximately two hundred dollars, and we spent almost all of it. A day or two later, my mom said to me, "Lou, if you and Irene want to stay here, I want twenty-five dollars a week from you." There I was still in a cast from my ankle to my knee and couldn't go out looking for a job. It hurt a lot to hear my mom say that.

I had given her almost every cent I ever earned from the first job I started working right through all my years in the service, and also while I worked for the government. When I first left school at sixteen and started working, I was making twenty-five cents an hour. But as the years went by, I got better-paid positions. At age nineteen, I was working at a defense plant earning fifty-five dollars a week. After entering the army, I enrolled in the allotment program where the government took part of my monthly pay and added more money to send to my parents. There were many times I would still have money left over at the end of the month. I sent almost all of my monthly income home. I sent my parents a thousand dollars just before we left Germany, knowing we would be staying with them for a short period of time until I found work. Now I was busted, no job, my leg in a cast, and Mom wanted twenty-five dollars a week. What a homecoming!

Thank God the government had a program called 52/20. This meant if you had been in the service, you could apply for twenty dollars a week for up to fifty-two weeks if you were unemployed. I applied, and as soon as the checks arrived, I gave them to Mom.

It was very difficult for Irene, since she did not speak English at all and Mom did not like her. Why, I don't know. I think it might have been that Mom blamed Irene for the trouble I got into while in the army, and because I didn't come right home after the war was over. Irene felt awkward around Mom because Mom ignored her. Although Irene was always doing everything for me and the rest of the family, Mom was indifferent toward her. So long as I was there to protect Irene, she felt secure. She more or less accepted Mom's attitude toward her. As for my pop and brothers and sisters and other relatives, they all loved Irene except Mike and, of course, Mom.

Because there was no German spoken at home, Irene had to learn English. Between the TV shows and going to the movies with me, the words started to come together for her. There are quite a few German words that sound similar in English, and Irene picked up the English language very quickly. Shortly afterward, she even started to read English, too.

One day, my eldest brother Andy came to visit us and was having fun with Irene by asking her to say different words in English. After a few minutes, he asked her to repeat a certain phrase. You guessed it, a curse. Irene didn't know what it meant, so she repeated it. The words that she uttered were "son of a bitch." Andy laughed so hard because if you ask a foreigner to say a curse word, it sounds so cute. We all had a few laughs at Irene's expense.

After a few weeks, the doctor removed my cast, and it was now time for me to look for work. Two years after the war was a bad time to be coming home and looking for a job and a place to live. All the places to live were taken, and all the decent jobs were also taken. The only thing I could do at that time was paint spray. Of course the wages for that were not too good. My younger brother Frank had gotten married in September, and my aunt had promised him the basement apartment at her house, so again I was out of luck. The country had changed a lot since the war.

One of my friends who had worked with me in Germany now lived in a Manhattan apartment, and he knew I was looking for work. He asked his next-door neighbor, who was a foreman on the waterfront in lower Manhattan, if there was anything available for me. The guy had a regular crew that would unload all the bananas from the ships arriving in New York. I was told to be at the dock the next morning. I met with him and he hired me. The men would open all the hatches at every level of the ship and put in a conveyer belt to the top. Starting at the bottom of the ship, I worked unloading the bananas with the other men. We would flip the stalks onto our shoulders, take them over, and flip them onto the conveyer belt. When all the levels were empty, we would unload the bananas from the deck to the docks.

My problem was that these bananas were dark green and very hard. Every time I picked up the stalk, it felt like sandpaper on my shoulder. It did not take long before I was bleeding. So I changed shoulders, and by lunchtime the same thing was happening to my other shoulder: cut up and bleeding. Well, I found out that the rest of the crew all used heavy pads on their shoulders. Not one of them told me about the pads, much less let me borrow any. At lunch time, I was bleeding and in pain, and I went to the foreman. I apologized for not being able to complete the day, but I was in a lot of pain. When I arrived home, Irene was surprised and shocked to see me like that. She cleaned and bandaged me up, and within a few days I was fine again.

I had to look through the want ads every day for work as a paint sprayer, since most of the jobs I got were only temporary. The paper would arrive at the candy store at 9:00 a.m. and by the time I called a place, the job would already be taken. I realized that I needed the paper earlier then the candy store received it. So I decided to go directly to downtown Brooklyn where the papers were delivered between six and seven o'clock. Irene came with me, and we left Mom's house at six. We took the train downtown to pick up the paper around seven. If I saw an ad, I was able to call before seven thirty, and as a rule, by 8:00 a.m. I had the job.

Irene all ready to go to my brother Frank's wedding
Brooklyn, NY - September 1947

Mom would go to the movies a few times a week and would leave Irene home to clean the house. Irene became the *putz frau* (cleaning woman) for the entire house. There was much tension at that point because I did not approve of the way Mom was treating Irene.

One day, Mike and I were having an argument, and it ended up in a physical confrontation between us. It all started in the kitchen, where Mike, Irene, and I were eating. Mike said something derogatory to Irene, and I told him to be polite toward her. He then said to me, "Why don't you and that Nazi bastard get the hell out of this house?" That is when the fight started. It escalated from the kitchen to the dining room. Mike was bruised and bleeding. He went upstairs to wash up. I went after him and tried to apologize, but he refused to accept it. We started fighting again.

When it was all over, Mom ordered me and Irene not to come down from our bedroom and never to eat with them in the kitchen again. Anyone would have said, "Lou, why don't you find your own place to live?" I felt the same way, but I still could not find a steady job to pay rent on our own apartment.

Since we were not allowed to come down to the kitchen to eat with the rest of the family, I bought a small, tabletop electric stove with a heating element to make coffee in the morning. It was November, and Irene was able to put the milk out on the window ledge to keep cold. Irene would meet me at a diner at night when I got off the train, and we would have dinner. I wanted badly to leave my mom's house, but at the time it was impossible. Irene remained strong, never complained.

Well, things at home went from bad to worse, and Mom told me to find another place to live. I was taking home about thirty-two dollars a week and I couldn't afford to rent an apartment. My father had a friend who owned a real estate store, and Pop asked him if he had any cheap apartments to rent. There was a one-room basement with no kitchen, just a slop sink. The owner had put a stall shower next to the leaky oil tank. It also had a small stove. When my pop mentioned this to me, I thought I could never afford the rent money. He said the landlord wanted forty-five dollars a month. I decided to rent the apartment, just so we could have our own place and be out of my mom's house.

It wasn't much, but it was our own, and it was the first time we had been alone since coming to New York. Irene was very relieved that we no longer lived with my mom. Now she could set up her own housekeeping and not be ordered around anymore. Irene was truly happy now. We struggled, but we managed to pay the rent each month.

Approximately a year later, Irene became pregnant with our first child.

Our Bundle of Joy

Now that Irene and I were going to be parents, and we were broke, I had to borrow money from my siblings again to pay the hospital and doctor bills. Every time I managed to get out of debt, something would turn up and I would end up in debt again, having to ask my siblings for a loan. Since Irene and I had arrived in the United States from Germany, we hadn't had much money, and it was difficult to make ends meet. Andy was really pissed at me. He wouldn't lend me any money because he thought I was a good-for-nothing bum and would never amount to anything.

Things were bleak for Irene and me at this time. During Irene's pregnancy, we discovered the entire basement apartment was turning green from mold. Not only the apartment itself, but everything in it, including our clothes and shoes. When Irene told the doctor about the mold, he said to look for another place to live immediately because it could affect the health of Irene and the baby.

A woman who owned a restaurant on the corner knew a German couple on Eighty-Fifth Street and Sixteenth Avenue who were fixing up a small apartment in the rear of a two-family house. The entire apartment was twenty feet by twenty feet. We went to visit them and he was delighted to meet Irene. He told us he would have the apartment completed within a month. He was asking forty-five dollars per month plus gas and electric. We agreed to rent the apartment, and we terminated our agreement with the owner of the basement apartment. Then we moved to the small apartment on Eighty-Fifth Street.

At that time, when a woman was in labor but before she gave birth at the hospital, the doctors would tell the father-to-be to go on home and wait, the hospital would call when the baby was born. We didn't have a car or telephone, so I gave them the number of the landlord's daughter to call. She lived in the front house. After I got Irene to the hospital, I took the bus home. I asked the landlord's daughter to notify me when the hospital called, so I could go back to see Irene and the new baby.

Well, Irene gave birth to a beautiful baby girl, Celia, early in the morning of October 6, 1949. The hospital called the number, but I never received the message. At 9:00 a.m., I went to the gas station where there was a telephone and called the hospital. They said they had called, and wanted to know why I had not come to see my wife and new baby girl. I jumped on the bus and went to the hospital. When I arrived, they were still looking for an answer as to why I hadn't come earlier.

When I finally got to see Irene and the baby, I was thrilled to be a dad and Irene was thrilled to be a mom. It was a wonderful feeling, being a parent for the first time and looking at my child and seeing how small and helpless she was. After viewing the baby in the nursery from behind the glass window, I went to Irene's recovery room, kissed her, and asked her how she felt. She said, "I am fine, but did you get to see the baby?"

I answered, "Yes, I did, and she looks wonderful."

Irene looked a little tired, but she was also happy to be a mom. I visited with her and the baby each evening after work. After six days, they both came home. Pop drove me to the hospital on the day Irene was discharged. It was more convenient that way.

Backtracking a Little

When World War II ended, the government started a program to give returning veterans the opportunity to further their education by going to college or job training in a different field. When my brothers Mike and Frank came home from the war in 1945, they both worked at odd jobs. Sometime in 1948, Mike decided to reenlist in the army. Frank, who was always a whiz in electronics, decided to enroll in the government program for job training in radio and television.

I myself also enrolled to learn carpentry. I really can't recall how many evenings I went each week, and to be honest, I wasn't learning anything at all. There was no teacher to show us how to use the tools and machinery. So after some time, I decided to leave that program.

Frank stayed on and graduated with high honors. He started working as a television repairman at a local store that sold appliances and televisions. He also tinkered with radios in his spare time. One day he asked me to join him in lower Manhattan, where he wanted to buy radio tubes. There was a bookstore next door, and we went in to see if he could find a book on radios and televisions. I noticed a large table with a lot of books. One of the titles was *The Art of Furniture Finishing*. What made me pick it up and buy it, I don't know, but I changed my career just by reading this book. It turned my entire life completely around.

Frank eventually started his own business in 1952 or 1953, repairing and installing television sets. After three years, he quit the business, and in 1956 he and his wife decided to move to Florida. They did not have any children, and he had many enterprises that he was involved in. He started working as a troubleshooter for a firm that made ship to shore radios. He had to board all kinds of boats and yachts in South Florida to repair their radios when they couldn't receive any transmission. From there, they brought him into the shop as a plant manager, and from there he was made vice president of the company. However, Frank never felt comfortable sitting in a large office and having to make decisions on matters of the company's welfare. After four or five years, he felt it was time to move on. He started another business where he bought and repaired cameras. He made jewelry and his own furniture. He was a very talented guy. He also could sing and play the guitar.

After Cecilia was born, we bought a crib to place next to our bed. It was a small room and everything was tight. She was a good, healthy baby, always content playing in her crib with her toys. Whenever Irene would take her to the doctor, he would always comment on how great she looked.

When she was six months old, we needed to buy a high chair for her. I couldn't scrape up the money, so again I had to borrow. At that time there was a company called Household Finance. We borrowed twenty-eight dollars from them and had to repay a dollar a week for thirty-two or thirty-three weeks. This company really helped a lot of people who couldn't afford to pay cash for any purchases, and there were many people borrowing from them.

I was working as a sprayer of small, wooden frame clock cases. After working for the company for almost two years, I was laid off. I was never told the reason. It was tough working for small companies at that time, but I accepted what the owners did. Let's face it. They were the bosses and they had the final say-so.

Every time I would come home with my work clothes under my arm during the week, Irene knew I had either been fired or I had quit. It was tough for her. She never did complain, but I could see she was always worried about paying our monthly bills. She would encourage me by saying, "Lou, don't worry. We will always make do with whatever we have." As a rule, everyone liked Irene because she always tried to make people feel better. She had never been snubbed by other people. The fact is, they all loved her. She has made many friends throughout the years. Irene was always a great girl.

About a year later, when the doctor was checking Celia out, he said to Irene, "If you have another child within a year from now, I won't charge you for the delivery." That was really nice of him, but with our financial situation, we knew it would be almost impossible to have another child right away.

Trying Something New

After reading the book on furniture finishing, I decided to try working in that field. In 1951, I obtained employment in a furniture factory, spraying bedroom furniture. That was my first venture in the furniture business, but that job didn't last long. However, I liked the work and I wanted to learn all I could about it.

We bought a television from my brother Frank because he decided to get a larger set. It was more or less a gift from him, and we enjoyed watching it. I enjoyed the boxing events every Friday night. I think they called it *Pabst Blue Ribbon Friday Nights at the Fights.* They had some great fighters back then. Irene never liked boxing, but when I watched baseball, she would ask me questions about how the game was played. She enjoyed watching the batters hitting the ball and running to the bases. It took a little while for her to understand the game, but she learned to enjoy watching it.

She asked me what team I rooted for, the New York Yankees, the Brooklyn Dodgers, or the New York Giants. She wanted to root for a team, too. I told her to root for any team except for the Brooklyn Dodgers. She said, "Okay. I'll become a Giants fan." There we were, living in Brooklyn and rooting for the Yankees and the Giants. There was a lot of rivalry between the fans of the New York teams, especially between the Dodgers and the Giants.

In 1951, the Dodgers and the Giants were in a playoff for the National League pennant at the Polo Grounds. The Dodgers needed two more outs in the ninth inning when the Giants' Bobby Thomson hit a home run and the Giants won the Pennant. They called it "The Shot Heard 'Round the World." Irene watched the entire game on TV that day, and she was so nervous that she kept leaving the living room and walking into the kitchen, then back again to watch the game. She was thrilled that her Giants beat the Dodgers that day.

Later on that day, Irene took Celia in the carriage to do some shopping. They walked along Eighty-Sixth Street between Eighteenth and Twenty-First Avenues in Bensonhurst. She said she watched all the

Dodger fans screaming and crying and shouting how they couldn't believe their Dodgers lost that game to the Giants. And there was Irene, pushing the carriage, so proud her team had won and happy she had watched the entire game on TV. From then on, she was hooked on baseball and the New York Giants.

In 1957, our beloved Giants, along with the Brooklyn Dodgers, decided there was more money to be made by leaving New York and moving to California. So after the 1957 World Series, the two teams left New York for good. The Dodgers became the LA Dodgers, and the Giants became the San Francisco Giants. The New York fans were truly disappointed that their beloved teams had deserted them for California. We still rooted for them for a while anyway. Then, in 1962, something wonderful happened. A new baseball team came to Queens. They called themselves the New York Mets. Now we had another team in New York to root for. Many New York baseball fans decided they were going to became Mets fans, including Irene.

In Brooklyn, along Coney Island Avenue, there were several furniture refinishing stores that would take old furniture, strip it to the bare wood, and refinish it to look totally new. I would buy the daily newspaper and look in the want ads for that type of work. One of these stores was looking for a finisher. I applied and got the job. My new salary was forty dollars a week, and my take-home pay was thirty-two dollars. I explained that I knew how to spray lacquer and I wanted to learn all aspects of the trade.

In the 1950s, most people had wooden kitchen sets. It was popular to refinish them rather than buy a new set. My boss had a large vat with paint remover liquid in it, and my job was to dip all the wood chairs, tabletops, and legs in the vat and let the remover soften the lacquer before I scraped off the old finish.

I wanted to learn the finishing business from the top to the bottom. My boss was a real professional at finishing furniture. He could grain and marbleize as well as finish the wood. I told him how much I wanted to learn the business and that I was willing to start from the bottom up. It's funny, but the old-timers would not teach the younger workers. Why,

I don't know. My boss would only let me strip the wooden furniture, except occasionally when I would spray lacquer. Whenever I asked him to teach me to stain and glaze, he would ignore my request, and I knew I was not going to learn anything from this shop. I approached him one day and told him if he wouldn't teach me anything about the business, I had to move on.

It was 1952 and I'd been home for five years now. I was still struggling and borrowing just to make ends meet. I felt sorry for Irene; she never complained once. She understood what I was going through. In the previous five years, I had had many menial jobs, and almost all were temporary. I kept cutting out the want ads that advertised for furniture finishers. One was even a two-month-old ad for a repairman for television cabinets. I called anyway. Sure enough, the manager asked me to come in for an interview.

That company was CBS Television. Yes, *that* CBS Television; in those days, they manufactured televisions as well as creating television shows. I'm not sure of the exact address now, but it was a large building on Fifty-Third Street in Brooklyn. I was very excited about it, hoping this would be my first real break. At the interview, the foreman explained what the job entailed. The cabinets were new but had chips and scratches that needed to be repaired while still on the assembly line. He asked me if I knew how to repair cabinets. My answer was, "Give me a chance to learn by having another repairman show me. After one week, if I can't do it, then I don't get the job."

He agreed, and I started the next day. After one week, I was ready to work on the assembly line where the TV sets ran on a conveyer. I was able to repair minor chips and scratches before the sets were put into cartons and shipped to the large department stores. Basically, this was only one phase of the refinishing business, but, it felt good having a steady job.

In 1952, Celia was three years old, and she had turned out to be a lovely little girl. She had blonde hair and blue-green eyes. When Irene dressed her up, she looked like a little doll. Now I felt we could afford to have another child.

On September 5, 1953, my second daughter was born. We named her Karin. This time I was able to pay the doctor and hospital without borrowing any money. That felt good. Irene had a difficult time with this delivery. The doctor used forced labor to help deliver the baby. Karin was a small child, about five pounds at birth. Thank goodness she was also a healthy child.

Living in an apartment that was twenty feet by twenty feet with two small children was tough, but we had to manage and we did. In 1954, our landlord's daughter moved out of the first-floor apartment in the front house. The landlord asked me if I wanted the apartment, which was five rooms. He wanted seventy-five dollars a month for it. I knew I could not afford seventy-five dollars, so I turned it down. He then advertised it in the paper, but was not pleased with the people who came to look at it. So he came back to me and asked, "How much do you think you can afford?"

I said, "Fifty dollars."

He said, "Okay, you can have it."

What a difference in the way we lived. It was just great. As time went on, I kept giving our landlord increases in rent every so often until I felt it was a fair amount I was paying.

1954, Brooklyn
Irene, Celia, and Karin

The End of an Era

In November 1953, my pop died from a heart attack. He was a small, thin man and was not a healthy man at all. He smoked most of his life. After the funeral, when things started to settle down, it hit me. Here was a man born in 1892, who lost his parents at a very young age, and had to wander the streets and steal food from pushcarts just to survive. He was self-taught with very little schooling, but managed to become an auto mechanic. He married and had seven children, went through the "Great Depression," lost his job, and saw three sons go off to war. He tried working in a defense plant, had to quit because of health problems, and finally died at age sixty-two. Who would want to live that kind of life? When I thought of Pop and his life, I cried. I don't think he knew what it was to enjoy anything on this earth. What a rotten life.

I dreamed about Pop many times, and I would ask him, "Pop, what are you doing here on earth? You are supposed to be in heaven."

He would reply, "No, son, I'm still here with my family."

These dreams were always the same and I really don't know why they kept repeating. Perhaps I felt he was at peace in heaven and then he could come down to visit his family. If only we could analyze our dreams and understand them. I do believe Pop is much better off in heaven right now.

When Irene and I left my mom's home, I decided it was best not to keep in contact with my mother because of the way she had treated Irene and me. I wanted her to know how I felt. So after Pop died and Mike reenlisted in the army, Mom was living alone. I asked Irene if we could have Mom over a few times a week and have dinner with us. Irene's reply was, "She's your mother, and if you want her over to visit with us, she's welcome." Irene never said anything bad about my mom. Even after all the abuse she took while living with her, she was just happy for me that Mom and I were getting together again.

I was happy also. I don't care how you say it, but you only have one Mom. It was wonderful of Irene to have Mom over for dinner a few times a week. It also brought Mom and me together again. In general, Mom was a lot more respectful toward Irene.

Whenever Mike came home on furlough, he and Mom would come over often to visit and share the days with us. Mike left the United States from time to time to be stationed in Germany and also in Japan. While Mike was in Heidelberg, Germany, I wrote to him and asked if he could possibly go to Geradstetten and visit Irene's mom and relatives to tell them that everything was fine with Irene and me. It was about eight years since we had left Germany together, and we were sure her parents would be happy to see my brother Mike. We knew they would enjoy updates as to what was going on in America.

Irene had been communicating with her relatives by mail since coming to America, but here was a chance for her brother-in-law to go visit her family and update them on everything in America. Irene wrote to her family, telling them that Mike would come visit and let them know how we all were doing. The sad thing was that Mike never went to see Irene's stepmom or family. To this day, I have never really understood the reason for his actions. Irene and I were very disappointed, but at the same time, Mike was Mike. Mike was quite independent, and perhaps he would not have felt confident visiting Irene's relatives. He did not understand German and probably would have felt embarrassed. Irene's family was very disappointed that he never went to see them.

Back at CBS Television, Arthur Godfrey had a show on the CBS network. They decided to advertise CBS Television's sets on his show. My foreman picked a table model, an open console model, and a console model with doors, and gave me the job of repairing them, spraying them with lacquer, and compounding them to a high-gloss finish. These sets were packed and shipped to the CBS studios in New York City.

On the day they were shown in the commercial, I went to the studio to clean and polish up the sets backstage before they went on air, making sure they looked shiny and new. This was when I met the entire crew of Arthur Godfrey's show. There was no need for me to go again after that, because the stagehands got the job of polishing the sets for each commercial.

In 1956, CBS decided it was not profitable to manufacture TV sets and shut down the plant. There I was again, out of work. The next day, I went to the employment office in Brooklyn, and they gave me the address of a shop that made architectural woodwork for department stores and wood paneling for executive offices and suites in new office buildings in New York and elsewhere in the States. I went for an interview and started work the next day.

This shop consisted of carpenters who would prepare all the woodwork and then wheel the pieces into the finishing room, where the woodwork was to be finished according to specifications. There were approximately twelve shops in New York City that did this type of work, employing about a hundred and twenty-five finishers, and we had to join the Painters Union to work there.

We stained, sealed, and lacquered or rubbed the paneling. Trucks would then deliver the woodwork to the new office building, where the carpenters would install it. I would then go to the building to fill in nail holes, do repairs and touchups on any damaged wood paneling, and polish it all up.

Most of these shops had a steady crew of finishers. Whenever a shop contracted a job and was running late, they would then hire extra help to finish the job. That's where I came in. I was what they called an extra. I worked at this shop for about three months on a special project, and when the project was completed, I was laid off. For the next five years, I worked at these shops on and off.

During those years, I also worked part time for furniture stores. As the furniture arrived in cartons from the manufacturer, occasionally it would be damaged. I would repair the damaged items before they were sent to the customers' homes. There were two stores I worked part time for, usually from 6:00 p.m. to 10:00 p.m. a few times a week. On Saturdays and Sundays, I would visit the customers' homes after the furniture was delivered and repair, touch up, and polish the entire set. I also was able to refinish furniture in the garage behind the house where I lived.

In 1961, the furniture finishers were not getting the same benefits as the painters in the Painters Union. If there was a holiday in any given week, the boss would lay us off for the entire week to prevent us from getting a paid holiday. Also, we had a seven-hour day, thirty-five hour week. Our bosses wanted us to work a straight eight-hour day at straight time. They received the okay from the union for a straight eight-hour work day. We were not getting any vacations, either.

In the summer of 1962, one Sunday morning after mass, Irene told me that the priest had mentioned that practicing birth control was a sin, but that it would be fine if she could find a doctor to give her all of the information regarding the rhythm method, which was approved by the Catholic Church at the time. After visiting the doctor, who performed an examination and asked some questions, he gave Irene a chart telling her when we could have sex safely on certain days of the month without birth control and without her getting pregnant.

Well, guess what happened? Within a few months, Irene found out she was pregnant again. Celia was thirteen years old, Karin was nine years old, and now a new baby was on the way. Irene cried, knowing it was going to be a hardship for the family to care for another child.

On May 9, 1963, I took the day off from work to take Irene to the hospital. As usual, they told me to go home and they would call when the baby was born. I received the call around noon that day and hurried back to the hospital. Irene had good news for me: the baby was a boy. Irene and the baby were doing well. He weighed in at ten pounds, eight ounces. And he was always hungry. After receiving his formula, he cried for more, and the nurses had to get more milk to keep him happy. We named him Gregory.

After two daughters, it was nice to now have a son. Irene was very happy knowing that I did want a boy this time. I was just elated. He looked so healthy and chubby. After bringing Greg home from the hospital, every evening after work I would go to his crib and just gaze at him. He was always hungry, and Irene had to boil his six bottles and nipples to sterilize them along with heating the milk every day.

One of the reasons I couldn't keep some of the jobs I had after coming home from Europe was that most of the bosses and foremen that I worked for were sadistic, miserable bastards. They loved to see the workers suffer, and they screamed and yelled, trying to make us feel inferior. Well, that did not work with me. I would tell them that I was equal to them, and if they didn't want to respect me as a person, I wouldn't respect them, either. I would either get fired or I would quit. Now you know the reason I had so many jobs. To this day, I can't believe how people with authority can be so sadistic and treat their fellow workers like non-people. If the situation were reversed, I wonder what their feelings would be like.

When Celia found out that her mother was pregnant with Greg, being a teenager, she was very embarrassed in front of her friends. But the day Irene and Greg came home from the hospital, she became the big sister, a teacher, and a big helper to Irene. Celia taught Greg to read and write by the time he was four years old. I was always proud of Greg and the girls. I remember Irene buying a jigsaw puzzle of the United States that had the name of a state and capital on each puzzle piece. Within a few months, Greg knew exactly where each state was located on the puzzle. He also knew the capitals of each state. Wherever we took Greg, he always read signs. Most people were shocked at this and asked where he had learned to read at such a young age. We explained that Celia spent many hours with Greg teaching him to read and write.

In 1965, I was working in the Bronx at an architectural woodworking firm. Celia, now sixteen years of age, graduated from New Utrecht High School in Bensonhurst, Brooklyn and enrolled at the State Teachers College in New Paltz, New York. She had always wanted to be a teacher. She studied French in high school and had decided that was what she wanted to teach.

Irene was fortunate in that she became friends with a few other German war brides who lived within a few blocks of where we lived. They got along well and would get together almost every day. These women and their husbands were no better off financially than we were, but they were one happy group.

From the time Irene and I started out on our own in that basement apartment, Irene made lots and lots of stews and lots of potato soup. She did her own baking, like bread; I loved her German Stollen bread. Her fruit pies are still the best, but I loved her cherry cheesecake, too. During the Christmas season, she made all kinds of Christmas cookies for the kids to bring to their teachers. The teachers loved them.

Irene always did the best with whatever she had to work with; whatever I could afford to bring home, she always made do. During the 1950s and 60s, some of my relatives were buying cars, homes, jewelry, and furs. Andy was always a boss or worked as a supervisor. He had a good income and would buy a home, stay a few years, sell it, and then buy another home. As for cars, Mike and Andy bought new Oldsmobiles during the 50s. Bea and Mom both bought fur coats. Ah, but Mom, she just adored jewelry and had many pieces of it.

The only thing Irene ever had were the two gold rings that her mother got for us for a few chickens back in Germany, one for Irene and one for me. But Irene never asked for anything or complained. Sixty-seven years later, Irene still wears the same gold ring. The inscription inside says *"Lou and Irene, Engagement – Christmas 1945."* Of course it is in German. Unfortunately, my ring split, and because of the work I did, I could never wear it.

Living in Bensonhurst and driving to the Bronx each morning was terrible. Traffic was awful. All the men in the shop asked if we could start at 7:00 a.m. The boss agreed.

When a new office building was erected in New York, usually a large corporation would occupy many floors, and at least a few of the floors were for executives. The executive floors had architectural wood paneling, including all the corridors, and every executive had a choice of what type of wood and finish he wanted in his office. All of this was arranged through the architect and the interior decorators. When our carpenters were almost finished installing the paneling, our shop would send a few of us finishers to repair the woodwork throughout the site. We would work closely with the architect and the interior decorator. When we were close to finishing the job, we would get a list of all areas that needed to be checked. Overall, we might have been on the job site for a few months. I ended up going out on almost every job, whether it was in New York City or out of state.

When I was sent to a job site out of state, for instance to Chicago, my company would buy my airline tickets and give me ten dollars per day to cover all my expenses. I had to rent a hotel room and have my three meals a day for the duration of the job, all on ten dollars per day. Even staying in flop houses and eating in slop houses, I still had to spend money out of my own pocket. There I was, a union member in the Painters Union, and the union made deals with our bosses as to what I should receive in expenses while out of town. Talk about sleeping in the same bed! There were times when I would be out of town for a few months. The bosses would not let me come home for a weekend. When the job was completed and I would complain to the union, you could be sure I would be out of a job the following day.

Going Back for a Visit

After Celia was born, I gave out cigars to friends and family. Irene took the empty box the cigars came in and used it for our expense payments. There was an envelope each for rent, electric, gas, and so on, and if there was a dollar or two left over when the bills were paid, she would take it to the bank. Throughout the years, this bank account kept growing and growing. In 1967, I was working steadily and bringing home a good salary, working seventy to eighty hours a week. We decided it was time for our family to go to Germany to visit Irene's family. At that point, it had been twenty years since Irene and I left. Believe me, I had never dreamed we could ever afford to visit Germany again.

Irene was a member of a German club in New York called Schwaben International. We were able to buy airline tickets to Germany at a deep discount through them. I think we paid $350 per person round trip. Celia did not join us because she was in college at the time. Irene, Karin, Greg, and I arrived at Stuttgart, Germany in August 1967. Irene was quite nervous throughout the plane ride. It was the first time my wife and children had flown in a plane.

Irene's family was waiting for us when we landed, and as we greeted each other, there were tears all around. It had taken twenty years, but Irene was home again. Irene's father had passed away in 1956, when he was 62 years old, so we were greeted by Irene's stepmom, her sister Marianne and Marianne's husband Artur, and their children. Irene's brother and his family were also there. Irene was just thrilled to be home again and see her family after all those years. I was also proud and happy to have done something that I thought I could never accomplish. What a wonderful feeling.

We remembered Geradstetten as a little village in southern Germany. We were completely shocked to see a four-lane highway running along the edge of the town. Many factories and new homes had been built on the outskirts of the village in the last twenty years. When I was courting Irene in 1945, Geradstetten was a village of approximately fifteen hundred people. It sat in a valley and had the highest church steeple in the entire area. It had many small plots of land for growing vegetables, fruit, and grapes for wine on each side of the valley. Most families owned some of this land. Irene's chores had been to do the house cleaning in the morning, then work in the fields to cultivate the vegetables and fruit that they owned. In those days when I went to visit Irene and she was not at home, the neighbors would tell me where in the fields she was working, and I would drive my jeep to her. She always had a kerchief on her head, a real country girl.

Most of that land was sold after the war for industrial purposes. It was strange remembering how everything had looked twenty years previously, only to find that nothing was the same as we remembered it.

While vacationing with Irene's family, we traveled to Innsbruck, Austria and a few other famous towns. Toward the end of August 1967, we said our goodbyes, and again there were tears all around. Irene was just thrilled to see her family again after all those years.

Staten Island

In 1968, after working many part time jobs for twelve years, I was now working full time, and we had saved enough money for a down payment on a home. We looked in Brooklyn but the homes were too expensive. The Verrazano-Narrows Bridge connecting Staten Island to Brooklyn had been completed in 1964. In our spare time, Irene, Karin, Greg, and I would drive over the bridge to Staten Island, and we would look at all the new communities and the new homes being built. We looked at a few models in New Dorp, and we liked a two-story detached home with a downstairs rental apartment and a full basement. They had just sold out the last section, but the builder told us that they were going to build the same models in a short time a few blocks away. He would notify us when they were ready to start building.

A short time later we were notified, and in the spring of 1968 we went back and picked out the model and the plot for our new house. We contracted with a down payment. The house was priced at $40,000, and there were some extras we wanted that added a few thousand dollars more. We had to put twenty percent down in those days. Irene was happy that we had bought a two-family home, since we could rent the lower floor, which had three rooms. That would help us pay off the mortgage. The builders told us it would take a year or maybe more before the house was completed.

Union Troubles

In 1969, the finishers from the shops were still not receiving all the same benefits the painters were getting, although we were all in the same union. The finishers went to the union officials and explained the situation. The union told us if we wanted to strike, then we should go ahead and strike. The next day we went out, but instead of the Painters Union supporting our strike, our bosses and the union agreed to let finishers from the Carpenters Union cross our picket lines and enter our shops to start working. Our bosses, the Painters Union, and the Carpenters Union were all in bed together. There we were, totally locked out of those shops.

While all this was going on, I was working for my company doing a job out of state at the university in Urbana, Illinois. Somehow, the union contacted me in Illinois and told me to return to New York. I ignored the order, and in a few days a representative from the Painters Union out there arrived on the job and told me I had to leave because we were on strike in New York.

When I came back to New York, I could not believe that we had been so terribly betrayed by all parties involved. There were a few shops who did sign new contracts to give their employees the new benefits, but only a few and not my shop. I had to join my co-workers and picket the shop every day or wherever our company was doing a job in New York City. Every other construction worker from New York ignored our picket signs and told us to get lost. We were 120 wood finishers who had belonged to the Painters Union and our own union did not support our strike. Neither did the Carpenters Union or any other union. That is the reason we were told to get lost by all the construction workers in New York.

One Saturday morning, I got dressed and went to an office building in lower Manhattan where my company had installed all of the architectural wood paneling for a large corporation. I wondered who was doing the repair and finishing of the woodwork while we were out on strike. I signed in at the front desk in the lobby, pretending I was a tenant there. I then took the elevator up to the floor where the paneling was being installed. As I entered the area, I could not believe my eyes. Our own painters from our own union were doing the work. Our bosses had made a deal with them to clean, repair, and refinish all the paneling on that floor. We were being shafted by every union in New York City. And they had the balls to call each union member "brother." Well, so much for the unions.

I managed to get a job with a shop that didn't strike. There was a large corporation moving into a new office building in midtown Manhattan. They were to occupy approximately fifteen to twenty floors. The company gave me a job working on this site until completion. I was on this job for a few months, and got quite friendly with the interior designer and decorator. She was very pleased with the way the job was going. I knew that when I finished this project, I would get laid off. And I was right; there I was, out of work again.

By this time Irene was starting to worry. Our new home in Staten Island was under construction, but it was taking a long time. I bounced around here and there doing part-time work where I could get it. Things were starting to get a little tight. Irene thought perhaps we had been too hasty in buying the house. From time to time we went to Staten Island, but there was not much progress on the house each time we went there. Then in August 1969, it was completed, and we closed on the house and planned to move the next week.

Two of my former co-workers rented a large truck on the morning of the move. Irene started to cry. I asked what was wrong. First she said she didn't want to leave Brooklyn and all her friends or our landlords. Secondly, she didn't know how to drive. Then she said, "I'm not going to Staten Island!" and she started to cry again. She felt like she was losing everything and everyone she loved. I promised her that if she still didn't like Staten Island in one year, then we would return to Brooklyn. She felt better after that.

We made three trips with the truck and we were all very tired. It was a very warm night, and we had no storm windows or screens in the house. The next morning, we all had many mosquito bites on our bodies.

We had advertised the apartment in the paper before we moved in, and about the same time as we moved, a young couple with a child became our tenants.

In the fall of 1969, Greg started the first grade in class 1-4. Irene was disappointed and asked the school administrators if they could put him in class 1-1. In the New York City schools at this time, the smartest first-graders would be in class 1-1, then the next smartest group in 1-2 and so on. The children in class 1-1 were considered the brightest and were taught more. Irene pleaded with them to test Greg before placing him. At first the teacher was not impressed with the thought. She explained to Irene that many parents try to advance their children to a better class. The teacher finally agreed to give him the test. Afterwards, she told Irene, "This boy can really read and write and definitely belongs in the smarter class."

In the first few months after moving, I still wasn't working. Irene was told by friends that there was a new department store opening on Hylan Boulevard and Tyson Lane. This was approximately one mile from where we lived. She never told me anything about it, and she with a few neighbors went there to apply for a position. They were all hired for ninety cents an hour.

Each morning, Irene had to take Greg to the school bus, then walk a mile to the store. She worked five hours a day, then walked back home to be there for Greg at three thirty when he came home. Irene was putting in twenty-five hours per week and earning $22.50 a week; after taxes, her take-home pay was a total of seventeen dollars. That doesn't sound like much, but back then it helped, especially when we were hurting. However, the job was only temporary for the winter holidays, and right after Christmas, 1969, she and the other women all got laid off.

Within the first few months of living on Staten Island, Irene and I made many friends. We had block parties, barbeques, and social get-togethers with our neighbors. Irene was always busy at home, and she became quite comfortable living on Staten Island. Her girlfriends from

Brooklyn would come occasionally to visit, and she was always happy to see them.

For the next few years, I worked on and off, but I could not find full-time employment anywhere. Then one morning in 1972, I got up out of bed and sat on the edge and said to myself, "Lou, you have to do something real quick or you will lose the house and everything you ever worked for." I made my mind up: I had no other choice but to start my own business.

I went to the local bank, sat down with the manager, and asked if he could start me up with a business checking account. Since I still had a few dollars in that bank, he agreed to help me. Okay, that was one down and a few more to go.

Next, I went to a print shop and told him I wanted five hundred business cards printed. Two down.

Next, I asked my accountant if he would handle my business account. "No problem," he answered. Three down.

Then I contacted my insurance agent, and he agreed to insure my business. Bingo!

The name of the company was American Woodcraft. I paid a visit to the interior decorator who I got to know while working on that large office job in midtown. I told her that I was starting my own business. I wanted the job of maintaining all the architectural wood paneling in the two upper executive floors of the company we had both worked for. She gave me a general idea how to write a proposal. I then went to the company and sat down with the manager of office services. I showed him my proposal. He agreed to have me come every Saturday and Sunday to repair and do maintenance on the paneling for the two executive floors, to be completed within one year. I asked one of my ex-co-workers if he would work with me on weekends. He agreed.

That was the beginning of a long adventure, which was to include many things that I did not understand at that time. During the week, I went to the city and looked at the directories in each large office building. If a company occupied five or more floors, I presumed they had executive floors with wood paneling. In those cases, I would try and meet with the manager of office services, give him my card, and express the hope that he would give me some work in the near future.

The managers always asked me how many other accounts I had. I always told the truth, since it was better than being caught in lie. I answered, "At this time, only one."

Another question always was, "How much money do you have in your business accounts?"

I would answer, "I am just starting this business and I don't have anything yet."

It looked like I had three strikes against me before I even got started, but some of the managers asked me to refinish a desktop to see how good I was. That helped me a lot, because they could see I did fine work. Given the chance, I could handle any type of finishing. At the beginning, I worked mostly by myself and never had problems with any of the jobs.

Of course, there were many times I could not even get past the receptionist. Many of the companies already had contracts with other furniture finishing companies. But heck, I knew there was enough work out there for all of us; I just had to find it. I had so much confidence in myself and my work that I knew I was going to make it.

On one of my visits to New York City, I happened to encounter Eleanor Roosevelt in an elevator at an office building. What a spectacular coincidence. We just exchanged cordial greetings between the two of us.

In 1972, Irene, Greg, and I went back to Germany again to visit with Irene's family. I stayed two weeks and then came home alone to keep my business running. Irene and Greg stayed for one month. They really enjoyed being with her relatives.

In 1974, her stepmom was very ill, and the family asked Irene to come see her before the end. While Irene was there, her stepmom passed away. Now all the family Irene had left were her sister and her brother. She was very sad when I picked her up at the airport. Life does not end when someone you love leaves this earth, but it hurts a lot. That's when I decided it was time for Irene to learn how to drive.

At the time, I owned a 1969 hatchback Volkswagen with a stick shift. I then bought an American Motors Hornet hatchback with an automatic transmission. I gave Irene lessons, taking her out on the streets that were not too traveled. At first it was difficult for her, and she had trouble with her turns and judgment. I would get on her case at times, and then she would cry and say she didn't want to drive anymore and wanted to get out of the car. I made her continue, and she got much better with each lesson. She just needed a little confidence in herself.

After she took her test, she said the examiner complimented her on her driving ability and wanted to know who had taught her how to drive. When she said her husband, he was surprised. He said husbands were usually the worst teachers for wives. I have to admit Irene was a quick learner and is now a very good driver.

As time went on, I got a few small accounts, and at the end of 1972, I landed a contract with a large corporation in Manhattan to refinish many of their desks. That's when I decided to take on some help and hire some old friends who needed work. Fully self-employed, I had a room in my house that I used as an office. I set up a desk and office equipment like a conference table, typewriter, copy machine, business ledgers, and so on. Irene was my all-around assistant. She would answer the phone with her slight German accent and say, "Good morning, American Woodcraft." Many of my clients wanted to know what kind of accent Irene had; most thought it was Swedish or Danish. I had no problem telling anyone that she was a German war-bride. I was very proud to let them know it.

Irene also had to learn how to type. All my paperwork up to that point had been done by me by hand. She learned to type up proposals, invoices, and any correspondence I might have. With a lot of patience, she learned quickly. Of course, like any good secretary, she had her dictionary by her side.

One day, a company manager I was doing business with called me into his office and gave me some advice. He said "Lou, don't ever get too big that you can't handle all of the accounts." He suggested that I keep my company small so I could satisfy the clients when they called for service. He was right. I kept picking up more and more accounts, and sure enough, I received a call one day demanding that I send a few finishers over to a client the following day. When I asked if it could be in two days, he said, "If you want to keep the account, you better have the men there tomorrow." My men were tied up doing work at other companies. I couldn't release them to comply with this manager's demand. I called him back that same afternoon to apologize and let him know I could not have my men there the following morning. He told me that as of that moment, I had lost the account.

Still, as time went by, I was doing quite well. Some of the work had to be done in the evenings and some on the weekends, but the majority of the work was done during the regular work week. Most companies had space in the basements of their buildings for us to work. They would bring the furniture, like table, chairs, desks, telephone cabinets, and conference tables, to be refinished. Most weekends, I hired additional finishers to help with the work.

There were times when a company's CEO would retire and one of the board members would be chosen to replace him. The company would notify me and also the interior decorator to meet with the incoming CEO to discuss what his options were. Usually the incoming CEO would request the refinishing of the entire architectural wood paneling and have all his office furniture refinished. They asked me to make up some samples of finishes on different pieces of wood. Once the decorator and the CEO approved the sample, I would start the project within the next week.

One time, the entire project had to be done in the evening, and I had to be with the men as they worked to make sure everything went smoothly. The client wanted crown molding, chair rails, wainscotings, baseboards, wall units, and library shelves all refinished, and some of the furniture had to be stripped with paint remover.

At other times, we had metal furniture that had to be grained to look like the wood furniture in the room. To do this, you first have to spray the metal with a base coat. The base is a light tan color. Then you mix an oil glaze consisting of burnt umber and turpentine. This is applied to the surface with a rag or brush, and then a soft, dry brush is used to brush it out to look like walnut furniture. The final step is to spray it with clear lacquer. There is more to it, but that is the general way it is done.

A big problem we had was that in New York City, many if not most office buildings had windows that would not open. Also at night, when the regular office personnel left the building, the maintenance people would lower the air conditioning. We worked from 6:00 p.m. to 2:00 a.m.

You can imagine working all night stripping furniture in a closed space with no or very little air. Paint remover has a strong odor, and inhaling it all night really makes you groggy. When we left the building at 2:00 a.m. and went out in the fresh air, that's when it hit us. When I got to a lamppost, I just held on. Believe me, I would be really floating, and I could not think straight. There I would be in midtown Manhattan and I couldn't remember where my car was parked. I would hold on to that pole for a few minutes until my head started to clear up. After walking a few blocks to the garage where my car was parked, I felt better.

Through the years, I breathed in a lot of chemicals, and from time to time I felt a little tipsy from it. However, this was part of my profession. Yet, when I see a doctor today, he is usually surprised that my lungs are in good condition. Perhaps it's because I never smoked. However, I had many headaches during my life, and I still have them.

Shortly after Celia started teaching high school French classes in 1969, she met a local boy from New Paltz, New York named Jim Cornwell. As a rule, Celia would come home to Staten Island most weekends. She asked Irene and me if she could invite this boy to visit with us. We were anxious to meet him. One weekend Celia brought him home, and we liked him from the start. After a two-year courtship, they decided to marry. In June 1972, all the family and relatives were invited to their wedding which took place in New Paltz. The wedding reception was held in a country restaurant and bar overlooking the Hudson River. It was a beautiful day, and everything went great. Irene had a beautiful yellow dress on, and all of Celia's friends thought she was Celia's older sister instead of her mother.

Our son Greg was now nine years old, and he was into hockey. He loved to watch it on TV, and he followed the standings of all the teams. He asked me to buy him a hockey stick and puck so he could play in the street with his friends. A few years later, around December 1975, I bought two tickets for us to see the New York Rangers play at Madison Square Garden. We were seated in the upper section (Blue Section), and I was sitting on the end of the row next to the steps. As the game started, I couldn't believe what I was seeing and hearing. All the fans were screaming for the players to start a fight with one another and were looking for blood. As the game went on, a fight did break out between two of the fans a few rows up from us. All the fans were yelling *kill him, kill him.*

The fight spilled out on the steps, and they rolled down to where I was sitting. I got up and struggled with the both of them and finally managed to pull them apart. As they were throwing punches at one another, I got hit a few times, but I was not hurt at all. Finally the security guard came and told the two men to follow him to the security office. About fifteen minutes later, back came one of the men. As he approached me, he stopped and shook my hand and thanked me for breaking up the fight. He said that the other guy had been giving him some beating. If I hadn't come to his aid, the other man would have severely injured him.

I can't understand the logic of fans who fight while watching a sporting event. Personally, I think they are all sick. After the game, I approached the security guard and asked him why he didn't stop the fight. He said that at every hockey game he sees many young men fighting among themselves and doesn't even try anymore to stop them. He said, "If they want to see blood, then let it be theirs."

That was the first and last time I took Greg to a hockey game. If that's their idea of sportsmanship, they can have it.

During the 1970s, my business kept me busy and from time to time I had a problem or two with the Painters Union. When I started my company, I promised myself that I would not have anything to do with any union. That meant mine was a *non-union shop*. In general, I had no problems with any of the jobs we did in New York City. But occasionally the Painters Union would try and give me a hard time. There were times when they would go to the building manager and tell him if my crew didn't stop working and leave the building, the union would set up picket lines in front of the building. That would often be enough to scare the heck out of him. He would ask my men to leave.

Why were some of the owners and managers so frightened of the unions? All they had to do was say that I had a written contract; I had the right to work in that building. It amazed me how the unions could stop me from earning an honest living.

I had quite a few confrontations with the unions, and it only made me more bitter toward them. Before I started my own company, I was a member of the Painters Union for almost fourteen and a half years. When I turned sixty-five, I applied for a union pension. Guess what I got? A letter informing me that I didn't have enough years in the union to receive a minimum pension. My workers received between two and four weeks vacation, paid holidays, a health plan, and a pension plan. Their hourly wages depended on their experience and ability, not on their seniority. It was a lot more than I ever received from the union as a paying member. I still can't believe how much control the unions have.

About now I was fifty-eight years old. My daughter Karin, who was working for JC Penney, transferred to their Woodbridge, New Jersey location as a merchandise manager and buyer of children's clothing. There, she met her husband Tom, and in 1985 they married. They settled in Shark River Hills, New Jersey, where they bought a house. They had their first child Kerry, the following year, and their second child Lexie was born a few years after that.

In 1980, I decided to go back to school to earn my high school equivalency diploma. The state had evening classes that were open to everyone. After registering and getting my schedule, I started evening classes. There were many young people there. Settling in my seat, I looked around and noticed I was the only middle-aged person in the class. They gave us students the program, which consisted of five subjects. I took those classes several times a week from autumn until the spring of 1981. When the classes ended, the teacher gave the students a schedule showing where the final test would take place, along with the time in the evening.

I remember completing all of the questions in every one of the five subjects on the test. There was no time limit. When I left the school building that evening, it was quite late. When I arrived home, Irene asked me how it had gone, and I replied, "The test was tough, but I think I did well." Now all we had to do was to wait for the results to come in the mail.

A month or so later, Irene came to me with the mail in her hand. She said, "Lou, I think this letter from the state may be what you're looking for."

I said, "Open it up and let's just hope I made it."

She opened it and there it was a high school equivalency diploma in the name of Louis Candela. Irene was so proud of me, and I was proud of myself, too. I had done something that I couldn't do as a young man: get a high school diploma.

The years were flying fast by then. Celia and her husband Jim, had a son Billy, our first grandchild, who was born in December 1976. In 1981, Greg entered Cornell University, where he met his future wife, Melissa. When he came home from college on the weekends, I would have him come out on the job with me. If I didn't need him, he would stay home in bed until noon. He liked that.

Greg liked history very much, and he told Irene that he would like to become a college professor teaching history. One weekend, Irene sat him down and told him the facts of life. She said that teaching was a fine profession but his income would be limited; then she suggested that he go to law school and become a lawyer. She told Greg about all the possibilities he could have and there would be no limit to how far he could go.

It didn't take Greg long to agree with his mother, and during his last year at Cornell, he applied to seven law schools. He was accepted by all of them. One of them was Harvard Law School. Irene and I were thrilled and said, "Greg you're going to Harvard, aren't you?" He said he wouldn't feel like he belonged in such a prestigious school because his mom had come to America not knowing the language and his father hadn't gone to high school. Irene told him that the school didn't care where or how far his parents have gone. The most important thing was that he had been accepted because of his academics and his achievements, including being president of his fraternity at Cornell. He did decide to go to Harvard, but said he would feel out of place there because of all the wealth that went with it.

1972
Jim & Celia's wedding day

Irene with our first grandchild, Billy
1979

Retirement

I was thinking about retirement when Greg was in his last year at Cornell. I was sixty-three years old then, but when he decided to go on to law school, I knew I had to work a few more years. In the years since I had started the business, some of my customers had moved their headquarters to other states and I would lose their account, but I always managed to acquire new accounts from other companies. I was very fortunate in that many new accounts were from referrals from my previous clients.

In 1985, Greg started law school and that first year was really tough. The second year was a lot better. At the time, I was telling all the office managers I did business with that I intended to retire in a year or so. I said if I could sell the business, the new owner could continue with all the accounts. The word got out, and I received a call from an owner of a maintenance company. They cleaned and polished brass doors and the fronts of office buildings, including the marble floors and walls. I met with him and he was very interested in acquiring my business. Greg still had one more year of law school to go, and I assured this gentlemen that when Greg graduated in 1988, I would be retiring.

During my last year, I acquired accounts from two large corporations next to the World Trade Center in lower Manhattan. It was a hectic year with so many accounts coming my way. I contacted the gentleman who was interested in acquiring my company, and we sat down with his accountant in my office. He wanted to look at all my books and records to see just how profitable the company was. The owner called the next day and wanted me to join him for lunch. At lunch, he agreed to the price that I was asking. I let him know that he was buying a good business.

In late 1987, I took him to lunch with every service manager of the corporations I had accounts with. By early January 1988, he had met with all of them, and each company agreed to let him continue where I left off. He agreed to keep all my finishers on his payroll.

Then came one of the happiest days of my life.

It's Final

On January 31, 1988, I met with my lawyer at his office in midtown Manhattan. I brought my accountant and all my records and books. The new owner arrived with his accountant. We agreed to a partial sale amount right then, with the remainder to come within the next two years. It was also agreed that I would work with him for the next few months whenever he needed me, just to help him learn the operation of the business.

After all the papers were signed and all the handshakes were shaken, my lawyer, Irene, and I went to lunch to celebrate my upcoming retirement. When we arrived back home, Irene and I kissed and embraced each other, and of course there were a few tears. I sat down on the couch and thought back to when I had brought Irene to America and couldn't give her anything the other women had. Somehow I still could not believe Irene had left her homeland and family to marry an American soldier who had nothing to offer her. Now, here we were more than forty years later, January 1988, and Irene and I were just thrilled knowing our working days were over. I couldn't help but think about my mom and brothers and sisters living retired in Florida.

From the first day we arrived from Germany, Irene had felt pressure from my mom. So it went for both of us. I got bounced around for years, getting fired or quitting jobs and always trying to make ends meet. I always believed I had someone from on high watching over me. He gave me the strength, determination, and lots of stubbornness to carry on. No question about it, I honestly believe He was with me my entire life, guiding me every step of the way. Yes, fate has been kind, but was it fate that sent me to Europe so I could meet and marry the woman who had stayed by me from the beginning? I remember telling Irene at Christmas time in 1945 about not having anything but my two hands and that we were going to make it. Now finally, everything was coming true. We had made it. Yes, that was one of the happiest days of our lives.

After World War II, my brother Mike, who was three years older than I was, worked for a few years and then decided to reenlist in the army as a career soldier. When the Korean War broke out, Mike was sent to South Korea and was seriously wounded. He ended up in a hospital in Japan, where his wounds eventually healed. He completed twenty years of military service, and in the middle of the 1960s, he was honorably discharged as a first sergeant. They recognized him with a parade and a gun salute. He was thanked for all the years he devoted to his country. Even though Mike and I had our differences, I was one proud guy seeing my brother with so many medals and hash marks all over his uniform.

Upon coming home to Brooklyn, Mike once again settled in with Mom. He had many girlfriends through the years, but only considered getting married to one of them whom he really loved. The problem was my mom; she didn't want Mike to marry *any* woman. She was the boss, and you can bet she was a tough woman, too.

My youngest brother Frank and his wife Gloria had left for Florida in 1956. My sister Min and her husband Charlie, along with their two children, had settled in Florida that same year. My oldest brother Andy with his wife Mae left for Florida in 1967, while Mike, after twenty years of military duty and living with my mom, also decided to settle in Florida.

That left my sister Beatrice and I still in New York. Beatrice was longing to be with the family, too, and in 1974 she and her husband Bill packed up and headed south to be with the rest of the clan. Beatrice's son Anthony, who remained in New York, worked for IBM, and finally he, too, asked for a transfer to Florida and received it. So by 1988, the entire family was in Florida except for Irene and me.

A short time later, Mike founded the Sunrise Police Reserves, a group of volunteers who worked with the police department in Sunrise. He rose to the rank of captain. When the young recruits were about to take their exams for the department, they would ask Mike to help prepare them for the test. Mike was well read on all things pertaining to police work, and he enjoyed helping recruits prepare for the exams.

Mike worked with the police department for twelve years doing various duties, like working with police officers on their paperwork, traffic direction, and crowd control. But in 1979, Mike came down with throat cancer. While he was in the hospital, Irene and I flew down to see him. He knew he was not going to live too much longer and called Irene to his bedside. He begged Irene to forgive him for his rudeness and for not being very social when he was with us. Irene and I said there was nothing to forgive, and all we wanted was for him to get well again.

A few months later, we received a phone call that Mike had passed away. I flew down for the funeral. He was just sixty-six years old. There was a police honor guard throughout the entire three days Mike was laid out. There was one policeman on each side of the casket from morning until night. Also the VFW came and held a ceremony in Mike's honor. I was watching all this every day and I could not believe all the honors that my brother had bestowed upon him. It was too much for me. Many times during the wake I had to leave the chapel; it was tough to control my emotions.

As kids, he would take me with him wherever he went. Everything changed when we all came home from the war. It was never the same again. It was not until I got back home to Staten Island from the funeral that I realized how much I was going to miss Mike. He was a funny man, told jokes, and enjoyed making people laugh.

My mom was now eighty-eight years old and living alone. Andy and his wife Mae suggested she sell her house and come live with them. She agreed and moved in with them, however, Mom asked Irene if it would be okay if she moved in with us. Irene agreed but said I would have to help out, because Mom could not do things for herself anymore and needed a lot of help.

It was amazing that Irene even considered having Mom live with us after the way Mom treated Irene and me when we first came home from Germany. Yet Irene put everything behind her and was willing to go along with it. When my other siblings found out about it, however, they were not pleased with Mom, and told her she would have to stay with Andy and Mae in Florida. They thought it best that Mom remain with them for her remaining few years. In April 1988, Irene and I decided to go to Florida and buy a house to use for the winter months.

When Mom was ninety-three years old, she developed some health problems, and after a few weeks in the hospital, Andy had to admit her to a nursing home. Shortly after that, Mom left us to be with the Lord. All of Mom's children were very good to her. Whatever she requested, the kids were always there to comply with her wishes. Her years in Florida were wonderful. She enjoyed the weather. We all missed her but were happy we were able to make her life on earth as comfortable as possible. I hope Mom and Pop are together again.

A Busy 1988

When my business finally got off the ground, we used to visit the family every year for a week around January 20, because that was Mom's birthday.

I honestly missed my family, and it was good to see them all again each year. I wanted to be near the family to do the things we had done when we were younger, like play games, tell jokes, laugh, sing all the oldies, and have a few drinks together.

As we were driving south, somewhere along I-95 in Maryland, I had to stop the car and get out because of a pain I was experiencing in my left buttock. I had no idea what it was, as I never had this problem before. The pain eased up and eventually went away. A few months later, it came back again. I asked the doctor what it was, and he answered, "Sciatica."

That was the beginning of eighteen years of back and leg problems. My doctor in Staten Island would give me treatments a few times a week which didn't seem to help much at all. The pain in my back side and legs would gradually recede and I would be fine for months, and later the pain would return again. In the spring of 2006, I had to give up golf and bowling altogether. I was having trouble even walking.

I tried other doctors and chiropractors, and finally I decided it was time to go for surgery on my back. I went to my family doctor. I said to him, "It's time," and asked him to recommend an orthopedic surgeon, who advised me to get an MRI and bring it to him. After looking at the MRI, he diagnosed my problem as spinal stenosis, or a narrowing of the spinal column. His office made arrangements for me to go on a specific day for an EKG and pre-operative test. In October 2006, I was operated on and it was successful. After three months, I was again playing golf with my buddies.

The irony of this whole story is that for eighteen years I suffered with this pain, when I could have had the surgery right away and it would all have been over within three months. There was only one way to relieve my pain, but it took me a long time to realize it. One of the many reasons I put it off so long was because I had heard so many negative things about back surgery. There was a chance that it won't work or I could be paralyzed or whatever.

Well, it's all over now and I'm in good shape. How does that song go by James Brown? "I Feel Good."

Getting back to our house-buying visit to Florida, we drove to Sunrise, where the family lived. They were happy for us that we were going to buy a house and stay, if only for the winter months. We bought a single-family home in Wellington, Florida, which is near West Palm Beach. It was scheduled to be completed in September 1988.

Also in May that year, my son Greg graduated from Harvard Law School. Irene and I drove up to Boston to see the event. The ceremony was outdoors, and it was just beautiful to see all the young students and their families gather for commencement. It was quite a thing to witness. Irene and I could not have been more proud of him. He did it all himself.

After we returned home, we decided it was time to leave Staten Island. We started looking for a home in Monmouth and Ocean Counties in New Jersey, maybe in a retirement community. After looking at many places, we chose Greenbriar Woodlands in Toms River, Ocean County. The houses were built by US Homes and there were 1,250 houses planned for the site. We picked out the model we wanted and contracted for the house to be finished in October 1988. We put our house on Staten Island up for sale, and in May we got a buyer but they were not able to move until the end of the year.

Since we were now retired, we had time for vacations and travel. So in July 1988, we left for Germany to visit with Irene's family. Irene hadn't been there in ten years, and I hadn't been there in sixteen years. We stayed with Irene's sister Marianne as a base and traveled around for a few days. Germany had been totally rebuilt. To think back about how almost every city, all the railroads, and the bridges that were destroyed during the war, it was amazing that everything had been rebuilt. They were even able to beautifully reconstruct some of the historical buildings because they had the original blueprints. The village of Geradstetten had grown, with new factories and homes. They also had erected a Catholic church. It was just amazing to see.

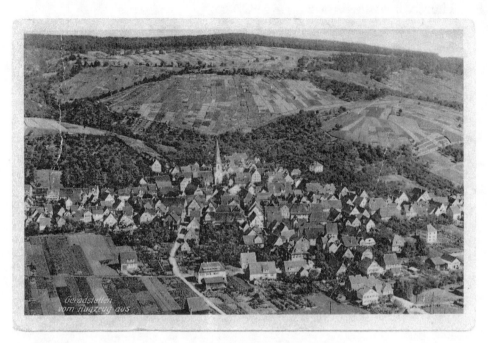

Irene's hometown,
the village of Geradstetten, Germany.
This photo was taken before WWII.
Lovely country in the south of Germany

Standing in the center of photo is Irene's father in the German army during World War I

Irene's father sitting at lower right side of photo. Note date of 1915 on sign.

Greg's Future

In the summer of 1988, Greg went to take his bar exam to become a practicing lawyer. It was a two-day exam, and within a few months he received a letter informing him that he had passed the bar. We were all excited and very proud of him. He specialized in litigation and soon afterward started at the firm of Dewey Ballantine (now Dewey & LaBoeuf) in Manhattan. He was living at home with us in Staten Island for a while, but then he wanted his own apartment in Manhattan. He chose a high-rise building in Battery Park. It was pretty expensive, between the rent, parking facilities, doorman, concierge desk, and all the maintenance people, not to mention everyone at Christmas time. *Wow.* He was just starting his career, and it was costing him way too much to stay at that location.

I suggested that he buy a house, and within a year he found a home in Ardsley, New York in Westchester County. He commuted to Manhattan via Grand Central Station. As all young people do today, Greg moved on with his career and is now with JP Morgan Chase in midtown Manhattan.

In 2004, Greg and his wife Melissa decided to move to another location in South Salem, New York. That is also in Westchester County, just a few miles from Ridgefield, Connecticut. They bought an old historical home that was originally built in 1763 on one level. Through the years, other owners had added to and remodeled the house, and today it is a two-level home. Greg and Melissa have added a new bathroom on the upper level.

In December 1988, Irene and I moved from Staten Island to Greenbriar Woodlands . We had closed on our new house in Florida in September, and in December we moved to New Jersey. After one week in New Jersey, we left for Florida for the winter months. We furnished the entire Florida house and it looked lovely. We had all the family from around Florida come and visit with us occasionally. It was good to be together again, just like the old times.

After a few months in Florida, though, Irene was missing the season changes and wanted to return to New Jersey. Florida has only two seasons: winter, which is nice, maybe cool; and summer, which is *hot* most of the time.

From 1989 to 1992, Irene and I would travel to our winter home in Florida. Irene did not care for the weather down there too much, and after three months of it she could not wait to go back to New Jersey. So I contracted with companies to maintain the Florida residence while we were not there, including lawn cutting once a week, insect spraying both inside and outside, and cleaning and maintaining the in-ground Jacuzzi on the back patio. Each month I would receive an invoice from these contractors for services rendered. In the summer of 1991, I received a telephone call from one of my neighbors down there. He told me that the companies that I had contracted with were not doing their job and the property was starting to look really bad. I was receiving bills for all their so-called work and paying them, and then I found out that the work had never been done.

I flew down to Florida that same week, and I was really pissed off at what I saw. The grass was high; it had not been cut in some time. The house had not been sprayed in a while and there were bugs, both living and dead, all around the inside and outside. The Jacuzzi was half-full of green, standing water with little frogs and slimy small eels and other small creatures in it. The bottom was all green slime.

When I called each contractor, they were surprised to learn I was in town because they knew I only came in January. The problem with owning a home in Florida and only staying a few months a year is that the contractors take advantage of you every chance they get. They then promised to take care of the house and get it in good shape. When we got back down in 1992, however, we decided to sell the place. When we wanted to come down again, we would rent. That summer I got a buyer who made an offer, and I accepted it. I lost money on it but I was just glad to get it off my hands. I chalked it up as a poor investment. I have to admit that after all the papers were signed and we were free and clear of the house, I was somewhat relieved.

September 1985 on their wedding day: Tom and Karin

Holding my granddaughters.
L to R: Kerry and Lexie in 1989.
They are Karin's two girls.

1991
Melissa & Greg on their wedding day

As I mentioned, our New Jersey home was in Greenbriar Woodlands. This is an adult community for ages fifty-five and over. There is a large clubhouse in the center of the community which has a lot of activities going on most of the time, such as ladies and men's card rooms, table tennis, bingo, drama club, camera club, and a ceramic room. If you like to paint pictures, we have a group that does that, too. There is a big main room for shows and dances, meeting rooms for clubs, and a lot more. We also have a large outdoor pool with a beautiful deck and lifeguards. There are three tennis courts and three bocce courts, and twelve shuffleboard courts too. The houses are built around the clubhouse, and it has an eighteen-hole, tough par 3 golf course with houses built along the fairways. We have a pro shop for our course with a PGA pro running it. We have a community association board handling the financial aspects of the community, and we have a private managing company to manage our grounds and other community business. There is a men's club that offers different activities, and a ladies' club with many more activities. When we have dances and socials, we get a chance to meet new neighbors who have moved in. We also have a lot of talented people who can sing and dance. They put on entertaining musicals and drama plays a couple of times a year.

I became a member of the golf club, and that is where I met some of my dear friends. I remember asking two gentlemen if I might join them. They replied, "Good to have you along." We introduced ourselves, and it was then that I met two of the nicest people in the community, Art Thomas and Joe Weber. Within a few weeks of meeting Art and Joe, I invited them and their wives to a social evening in my home. This is where Irene met them for the first time, Art and Sunny Thomas and Joe and Lillian Weber. We had a very interesting evening. They were asking Irene all about Germany. Most of all, they enjoyed Irene's German cake with chocolate icing. During the first few years around Christmas time, we would all welcome each other, and other couples as well, into our homes to enjoy the holidays.

In a gondola, Venice, Italy 1997
Lou and Irene

Irene at the Coliseum – Rome, Italy, 1997

Irene and I have been here now for over twenty-two years, and it's still a great place to live. The sad part is that from time to time, some of our dear friends have left this earth to be with the Lord and to have everlasting peace and happiness. It's tough, especially if you've been close to that person. We miss them, but we are happy we got to know them even for a little while.

We have lots of new faces here in Greenbriar. Many younger people (still fifty-five or over) are moving here. When Irene and I first moved in back in 1988, we would go to the dances at the clubhouse and know almost everyone. Now I can only recognize a few of the older faces. As the saying goes, "Time waits for no one."

We were lucky to visit with Irene's sister Marianne in Germany in 1991 and again in 1994. We stayed with her and enjoyed seeing all of Irene's relatives especially the younger children. For the first time in 1995, Christa and her husband Dieter came to the United States to visit us. They had heard about the Amish in Pennsylvania, and we spent three days in Lancaster. They couldn't believe how people could live that lifestyle and also speak fluent German.

When they left to return to Germany, they discovered that the airline they were flying with had to bump them off their flight. For the inconvenience, they got free round-trip tickets for the following year, and were able to return and visit with us again. This time we went to Washington, DC for three days and to New York City for all the sights. At the Twin Towers at the Top of the World, we got to see all of New York and New Jersey. We had a great time.

In 1997, 1999, and 2001, we revisited with Irene's relatives, and on each occasion we stayed with Christa. Irene's sister Marianne was then eighty years old and unable to have company and entertain people at her house. We were there for her eightieth birthday.

In 2001, my brother Frank passed away from cancer in Florida, and in 2002, our daughter Celia's husband, Jim, was diagnosed with cancer. It was too far advanced and there was nothing that could be done for him. They released him from the hospital right to hospice at home. He remained there for a few weeks and passed away at the age of fifty.

Jim was a man who lived for golf. His whole life was golf. I played many rounds with him upstate in New Paltz, where Celia and Jim lived. When his friends found out about his illness, they made arrangements at Pebble Beach Golf Course in California for Jim to play with them. It was one of his greatest moments for Jim to stand there on the eighteenth tee at Pebble Beach. Celia and I are grateful to his buddies for making Jim's last days so memorable. Yes, Jim was a good man, and everyone misses him.

At Greenbriar Woodlands, the men's league plays golf on Tuesdays, and on Thursdays we have a group that plays outside our community. There are many eighteen-hole, par 72 golf courses around Ocean and Monmouth Counties. The Greenbriar Golfers have been playing "outside" for many years, since 1987. It's been a lot of fun meeting and socializing with people from all walks of life.

Inside the Community, we also have our own VFW Post, Number 8885, with a monthly meeting. On Memorial Day and Veterans' Day, we have a parade here in the community. All the clubs meet, and we parade around from the clubhouse up to our main gate and back again. At the end of the march, we lay a wreath on a memorial stone and a bugler plays "Taps." Then we sing "God Bless America" and our national anthem. After, we go into the clubhouse for hot dogs and soda.

*Memorial Day parade at Greenbriar Woodlands.
For a bunch of old-timers, they look pretty sharp.*

Reflection

When I think back on my life and look at the world as it is today, I believe that my generation was the greatest of all. I am proud to have grown up during the Great Depression of the 1930s, from humble beginnings, without too many opportunities. Yet, trying to help our parents, giving them almost every cent we earned, going off to serve our country, coming home again, having to accept what was handed to us, and taking a lot of abuse, we still continued to get up every time we got knocked down. Only people who lived through that era can identify with me. That is why we old-timers can appreciate what we have accomplished in our lives.

Celia's daughter Andréa took classes in French during high school and became very well spoken in the language. In 2003, Andréa went to Paris and studied at the Sorbonne. While there, she met a French boy, Xavier, and they became friends. Back home, she enrolled at Binghamton University. Xavier came along with her and took classes in English at Binghamton. After graduating, Andréa went back to Paris to further her studies. She and Xavier had become very good friends by this point, and after Andréa returned home, he came to America to meet the family. We all liked him. He would help with anything that needed attention around the house. The problem was his French accent was so strong that no one could understand his English. He really tried, though.

Headaches

A short time after coming home from Germany, I started getting severe headaches. They kept getting worse as time went on. In the early part of 1950, a neighbor suggested I see a neurologist in Manhattan. This doctor took x-rays and theorized that the problem was migraine headaches. He gave me a prescription, and that was it.

As the years passed, the headaches got worse and it was a struggle for me to get up and go to work every day. When I lived in Brooklyn, I lived close to the new Veterans' Hospital off the Belt Parkway in Bay Ridge. One day I drove to the hospital because I was in such bad shape from the headaches. It was like someone was pumping air into my head, and the pressure kept building up. It felt like my head was going to explode.

I parked my car in the parking lot and could barely get out of the car. It took a while until I was able to reach the attendant at the information desk. I gave him my name and told him I was a veteran and I needed help badly. He asked what the problem was, and I told him about the severe headaches. Could someone in the hospital please help me?

His answer was that no one at the hospital could help me. I practically begged him to have someone give me painkillers or something to ease the pain in my head. He again answered that there was nothing they could do for me.

I couldn't believe what I was hearing. I surely thought the Veterans' Hospital was there to help all veterans who had medical or mental problems. There I was being turned away without help or anyone even looking at me.

I turned and walked out. As I approached my car, I opened the door and just sat there for about ten minutes with the pain in my head. I felt like crying. That was the first and last time I ever went to the Veterans' Hospital or had any contact with the Veterans' Administration. Since then, I have never bothered to ask them for any kind of help.

At that time, the only painkiller that I was able to get was plain aspirin. So for many, many years, I suffered with migraines headaches. Since I've retired, I don't seem to get them as often. When I visit the neurologist today, he prescribes painkillers and they help me. However, I don't think I will ever get rid of the migraines.

Thinking back on how my parents disciplined me and my siblings, I never had to do that with my kids. When they were young and got out of line, I would spank them. My eldest daughter Celia was somewhat defiant, and after a spanking she would say, "I don't love you anymore."

I would say to her, "You don't have to love me, but you will have to respect me."

Karin and Greg were really good kids, and I had no problem with them. Today, Celia is sixty-two years of age, and she tells me how thankful she is to have a father who watched over her.

Lou & Irene, Florida, 1981

Florida /The Villages

In May 1992, I rented a house in Central Florida in a place called "The Villages" in Lady Lakes for the month of March 1993. While there, Irene and I visited with my sister Beatrice for a day. She was over in Fort Lauderdale. Shortly thereafter, while we were still at The Villages, I received a call from Beatrice's son Anthony telling us that Beatrice had just passed away. I couldn't believe it; Irene and I had just been there the week before. She had seemed tired while we were there, but that's all. Anthony told me that she went to lie on the couch to rest a while and never woke up again.

Not only was it a shock, but it broke my heart. I remember when we were children, Beatrice was like a second mother to all of us. She would help Mom with all the chores at home and learned how to sew our pants and socks, which we always ripped and wore out. Bea never refused to help any of her siblings, and always tried to keep peace in the family right up to the very end. She was just a great sister, and I truly miss her very much.

Irene and I have continued to go to Florida each year and rent a home for the month of March. I play golf, swim, and try to get a good suntan. It's a very relaxing time for us to be out of the cold for one month of the winter. We have neighbors from Greenbriar who go to The Villages and also have homes down in Florida. Many of them stay for two to five months of the winter. It's funny; when Irene is down in Florida, she is looking to go back to New Jersey as soon as three weeks into our stay. She starts pressuring me to pack up to go home. We usually leave before the month's end.

There is a lot of traffic going north at the end of March; can you imagine how many cars and families leave Florida on the last day of March and head north on I-95? Believe me, it can be a horror story, especially when there are work crews repairing and paving stretches of the highway. You wonder where they got their brains from, doing that kind of work with so much heavy traffic. It seems they have no common sense.

When we do arrive home, Irene is happy that she can start her spring cleaning and garden planting. She plants tomatoes and flowers and watches her garden bloom and grow. Spring is always the nicest time of the year and is the most refreshing time also. When we are here in Toms River, our children visit with us from time to time, and naturally stay overnight or for the weekend. Celia comes from New Paltz; her daughter Andréa and her husband come from Washington, DC; Celia's son Billy comes from Brooklyn, and Greg and Melissa come from upstate New York. We have two bedrooms plus a sofa bed in the living room and one in the den. On Saturday night, Irene and I take out all the sheets, blankets, and pillows and lay them out on the living room chairs so our visitors can each decide where they will sleep.

When Irene and I come out to the kitchen on Sunday morning, everyone is still sleeping because they had a party the night before. We find empty bottles of wine and indications that they snacked, drank, and talked 'til all hours. My daughter Karin often comes by with her daughters on Sunday afternoon, and Irene has to entertain and feed the whole gang for the entire weekend. For the kids, it's a mini-vacation. Before they leave on Sunday night, they take whatever food is left and Mom's homemade cake if there is any to take. Overall, they really enjoy visiting with us. There's nothing like coming home to Mom's.

When Irene and I first came home from Europe, my mom showed her how to make Italian "gravy," and to this day, Irene's gravy still tastes like my mom's gravy—really good. When my children and grandchildren come to visit and stay with us, they are thankful to have a grandma who is so thoughtful, kind, and generous to them. Yes, I have to admit that my kids and grandkids are really a very lucky lot.

Whenever Greg is on vacation, he comes and stays for a few days. Of course Mom has to make his favorite foods—lasagna or ravioli with meatballs and sausage. He always brings a few bottles of expensive red wine. That goes well with Italian food.

Our daughter Karin and her husband Tom own an oceanfront sandwich shop in Belmar, New Jersey on the beach. It also is a hot grill and ice cream store all in one. It's located on Sixteenth Avenue across from the boardwalk. They work long hours seven days a week. So she doesn't get to call in to us too often, but she tells Irene, "As long as you don't hear from me, everything is fine." We hear from Celia often as she calls almost daily. Greg usually will call on Sunday evenings.

When Greg calls on Sundays, he and I discuss worldwide events, plus politics and how he is coming along with his company. When Irene gets on the phone, they start talking about (guess what) baseball. She and Greg can talk baseball for almost an hour. Naturally, it's about the New York Mets. It's amazing how much the two of them know about the Mets. She watches every game they play on TV, and every morning she reads the sports section of the papers to see the write-up on them. Who's on the disabled list, which players are not hitting well, which pitchers are not pitching too well. Irene and Greg feel sorry for them.

I have to admit I am not a sports fan. It's true when I was younger I did enjoy watching sports on television, but then reality set in. I had to worry about all the other things around me to help me make a go at life. I really don't care who wins or loses in any sport. So many people are so concerned about the well-being of athletes who earn millions and millions of dollars playing a game, the same game I played as a kid and I didn't get a cent for it, either. If I got hurt, nobody even said, "Poor Lou." Maybe it is a way for fans to relieve tension. They think they are actually part of the game. Who knows? Anyway, if it makes for good baseball talk, so be it.

A group from Greenbriar at The Villages in Florida, meeting for dinner at Nancy Lopez CC.
L to R: The Romeos, Morgans, Schnellers, Parduccis, Lathams, Hulbrocks, Hennessys, Coxes, Irene & Lou far right.
Seated: The Chalmers

Paris Revisited

In early 2005, Celia called and asked if Irene and I would like to accompany her on a visit to Paris for eight days. Andréa was there studying and working. We both agreed. It would be the first time Irene would visit the French capital.

Celia searched the Internet and found an apartment that was for rent in the heart of Paris. She made all the arrangements, and everything was set for a March visit.

As I mentioned, Andréa had a French boyfriend named Xavier, and she wanted to find out how he could visit America and how long he could stay. Andréa wanted to know because she was leaving Paris in the spring and starting law school at American University in Washington, DC.

Andréa and Xavier went to the American Embassy in Paris, and they were told that the best thing to do was to get married. Then they could come to the United States together and settle down without a worry about visas or how long he could stay. Celia called Irene and me and told us we were going to a wedding when we got to Paris. It was to be a vacation/wedding trip. Andréa and Xavier only had a month to put all the arrangements together and get all the things needed for the occasion.

A few days before we left, Celia said to me, "Dad, I understand that you never did get to see the Eiffel Tower or the Cathedral of Notre Dame when you were in Paris during World War II." I replied this was correct. She said, "You can forget about any *ooh la la* on this trip, because I'm making sure you get to see the sights this time around."

My reply was, "Aw, shucks."

On March 25, 2005, we left Newark Airport and went through all the formalities of boarding the plane to take us to a place where I had been many years before. When we arrived in Paris, Xavier met us at the airport and drove us directly to the apartment that we had rented. Andréa met us within the hour. The apartment was great: two bedrooms, a kitchen, a living room, and a dining room, with two small balconies.

Xavier had made arrangements for us to see different attractions and go sightseeing every day while we were in France. The first day, he drove us all around Paris. That evening, he took us to view the Eiffel Tower, where every hour for ten minutes the Tower would light up like a Christmas tree. What a great sight. All the traffic stopped and everyone in their cars emerged to look at the beautiful sight.

On the second day, Xavier and Andréa took us to Versailles, the Palace of Louis XIV. From there, we went to visit with Xavier's parents outside Paris. On the following day we drove to Normandy, where we visited first Le Caen Memorial museum. Any GI would have enjoyed seeing all the different features and the stories from World War II at this museum. Celia told the attendant that I was a veteran, and I was admitted for free. That was nice of them.

Then we visited Omaha Beach and the American Cemetery. There are 9,387 American soldiers buried at the American Cemetery. Irene, Celia, and I walked along the rows of marble crosses and read the names, ranks, outfits, and dates these heroes gave their lives. Other crosses that had no names read, "Here Rests in Honored Glory a Comrade in Arms Known but to God." The average age of the soldiers was twenty-two years old, a very sad sight to witness.

From there, we rode to Pointe Du Hoc. This was where US Army Rangers on D-Day attempted to scale a sheer cliff with rope ladders. Out of a total of 227 Rangers who participated in the assault on this cliff, only ninety of them survived. They were a brave group. Near this area was where the Rangers were supposed to knock out five German guns. However, the Germans had moved them to another area. I took photos of the gun emplacement and the small concrete bunkers at this site.

Overall, this day was something I will never forget. If only our government would be kind enough to provide for all of the remaining veterans of the D-Day invasion to go over there one more time and see how beautiful the cemetery is and all the museums that are in the area. Perhaps all the VFW organizations and the government could arrange for these old-timers to get one more chance to visit this historical sight.

On the following day, Celia took Irene and me to visit the Cathedral of Notre Dame. It was not far from our apartment, and we walked there. Once inside, I started a conversation with the priest who spoke fluent English. After we exited the church, Celia walked Irene and me to visit the archeological crypt that was on the same grounds.

The next day, we took the Métro from our apartment to see the fairgrounds at the Eiffel Tower. The lines of people waiting to go up the Tower were so long that we were surprised to find only one elevator out of four was open. It turned out it was spring break for American kids, and we realized that every kid from the United States had to be in line for the trip to the top.

We waited in line very patiently for two hours, and we still had about another hour to wait. Celia suggested we move on to another place, but I said that it was her idea to go to the Tower, and I for one was not leaving until I got to the top. It took three hours to get to the top, but I say it was worth the wait. It was the most beautiful sight of the entire city of Paris.

The next day we took the Métro again, this time to the Louvre. No matter where we went that week, there must have been thousands of American school kids at the same time, but the Louvre was beautiful, too. We got to see beautiful art: the Venus de Milo, the Winged Victory of Samothrace, and of course the Mona Lisa.

The big day arrived on Friday, April 1, 2005. Our granddaughter Andréa and her French boyfriend Xavier married in Paris. They had the marriage ceremony at the Town Hall that afternoon, and from there we went to Xavier's sister's apartment. We spent the entire afternoon and early evening eating and drinking cocktails.

At eight thirty, we left to go to the banquet hall where the reception was held. We got there about nine o'clock, and for the first hour we sat in the lounge area drinking and conversing with the young friends of Xavier, some of whom spoke English very well. Finally at 10:00 p.m., we went to the reception room and began dinner.

There were five courses on the menu. After finishing the first course, we went to the dance floor and danced until eleven. Then it was back to our table for the second course. This went on until 3:00 a.m., when we were finally on the dessert course. We were pretty tired at that point, and Celia called us a cab that came right away. We had to rush our goodbyes to Andréa and Xavier and the rest of the relatives and friends, because we had a flight for New York at eight thirty in the morning, and we had to get ready to leave for the airport.

We got to sleep for two hours before the cab came to take us to Charles De Gaulle Airport. As we boarded the plane and took our seats, I looked around, and again it seemed like every high school student in the United States was on that plane. I mean wall-to-wall kids. All and all the plane trip was not good. Those high school kids practically took over the plane, and they had all of their belongings everywhere. The aisles were all cluttered with their backpacks and books. It was an obstacle course just to get to the restroom. However, we accepted the fact that these kids were having a ball.

When we finally landed at Newark, we picked up Celia's car and headed for Toms River. Arriving home, we started to relax. It had been a hectic trip, but we were glad we made it. We got to see Paris together, and of course there was Andréa and Xavier's wedding. I enjoyed all the sights and especially enjoyed seeing Normandy. We were glad we got to travel with Celia, too. But we were still glad to be home again.

A few months later, Andréa and Xavier arrived in the United States. Celia helped find them an apartment via the Internet after searching for a few days. She finally found one in northwest Washington, DC. Celia, Andréa, and Xavier went to look at it. They liked it and agreed to rent it from the landlord on a yearly basis. In July 2005, Andréa started her first year at American University Washington College of Law.

Xavier, who had a green card and did not speak English too well, was an electrical engineer, but he was having difficulty finding work in that line. The problem was that in Washington, DC, most engineering jobs required you be a citizen of the United States. He sent out many résumés and visited many companies, but had no luck. He eventually went to work for a company that paid him very little and no medical benefits. Celia helped Andréa with her schooling.

In May 2008, my granddaughter graduated from law school, and in August that same year, she passed the bar. She is now working for the government as a lawyer in Washington, DC. Xavier, who is now a citizen, works as a computer engineer, also in Washington, DC.

Usually in Toms River, the weather in February is really too cold for golf or any other outside activity. Our golf course here in the community is closed for the month of February as "winter rest." On most afternoons, my friends and I meet in the clubhouse, where we either play cards or billiards. We kid around and enjoy a few hours of fun and laughter. We still have our informal dances and I look forward to them. When I hear the beat of the music, I just have to get up and do my thing. Of course I bring my bottle of wine, and by the time the party's over, I'm really feeling good.

Irene and Lou on top of the Eiffel Tower in Paris.

Irene and Celia at the Louvre Museum

The Caen Memorial Monument at Normandy, France

The museum near the Memorial Monument

Grave marker of an Unknown Soldier.
Unfortunately, there are too many of these crosses.

Normandy, France
The view: crosses of 9,387 US servicemen.

German gun emplacements at the beach of Normandy, France

Here we see underground bunkers.

Pointe Du Hoc.
At top left is a temporary monument where our Rangers scaled up the cliffs of Normandy

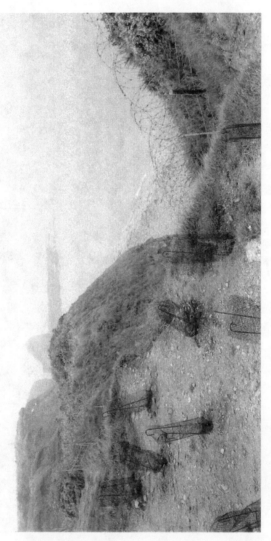

You can still see some of the barbed wire the Germans laid out by the beach.

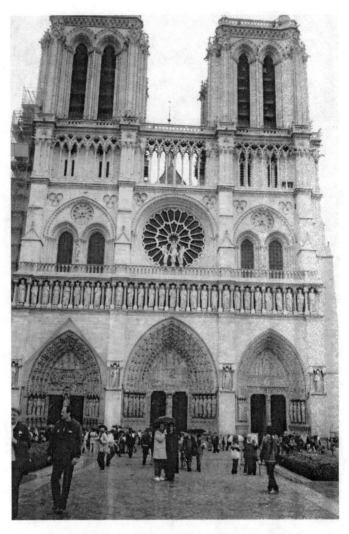

Irene and Celia standing in the rain outside
of Notre Dame Cathedral in Paris.
Construction was started in 1163 but was
not totally completed until 1345.

*Confessional booths at Notre Dame Cathedral.
Can you imagine how many people have
confessed sins in the past 700 years?*

***Xavier and Andréa
on their wedding day.
Paris, France***

At Andréa and Xavier's wedding
April 2005 Paris, France
Lou, Irene, and Celia

*Irene, granddaughter Andréa, Andréa's new
husband Xavier, and our daughter Celia*

*The car above on the left is the Mercedes
"Smart Car." They are very small, but
that's all you need in Paris.*

More Hobbies

When Irene and I first came to Greenbriar Woodlands, Toms River schools had adult education evening classes that included languages, carpentry, art and painting, computer classes, and so on. I took a course in Italian. I also took up duck carving and took three classes in it. I enjoyed that. I made a sandpiper and also three mallards. I hollowed them out so they would float when they were put on a pond or lake. It was a great, satisfying experience.

After that, I took some art classes. I painted a few pictures, but the only way I could become good at it was to dedicate myself to that. I noticed that the last couple paintings I made were getting better and the hand and brushwork were becoming easier to control and felt more natural. However, that also was years ago, and I have not gone to any more classes since.

I spend some time tinkering in my garage. When the weather gets warm enough, I take the cars out to have more room to work. I built a long workbench with a large vise, and I have all the necessary tools and machines for woodworking and repairing. I also set up a folding table at the entrance of the garage, where there is more natural light, and play my favorite cassettes. I love the old music from the thirties and forties. I have a lot of music, CDs and cassettes, of the Big Bands. Irene gives me a scotch on the rocks with a twist of lemon, and then I'm ready to do some work. I have everything I need: my hobby, my music, my scotch, and my Irene.

I recently bought a Bose SoundDock and an iPod that go together. It is a digital music system. I download my music from my computer to my iPod and I can listen to my many, many songs on it.

About eighteen years ago, I also started to repair my own golf equipment. I bought golf club components and assembled golf clubs. I also re-gripped clubs for myself and my friends. I realized that most putters I had bought were too light for me, so I decided to make my own putters. I make them from tubing that is either steel or chrome-plated. I melt lead, pour it into the tubing, and add an extension that looks like a "T." When I play golf, my buddies kid me about my heavy putter and the funny way it looks. Through the years, I have made many different putters, and typically I got many comments. All were negative. But as of 2009, all the putters you can buy on the market today are of the heavier variety. Now my friends say I should have patented my putters years ago.

I always felt it was more natural to hold a heavier putter than the lightweight original putters. A heavy putter creates a more pendulum-like motion, and you can control the club better. Truthfully, the reason I started to make my own putters was that I couldn't putt too well, and I believed it was because putters were made too lightweight. I developed the yips many years ago, and when I have a three-foot putt, I usually miss the hole. Now after all those years of making my own putters with special weights and taking the abuse from my friends, guess what? I still can't putt too well. I think I need a psychiatrist. No, really, just kidding.

Many years ago, I teed up a ball and hit it with my driver. I then saw the ball and the head of my driver going up in the air together in the same direction. I looked down, and all that was left was the driver shaft without the head. When I got to the head and picked it up, I noticed that approximately one inch above the hosel, or the point where the head connects to the shaft, the shaft had broken.

When I returned home, I heated the head and melted the epoxy with a propane torch. I pulled out the remaining three inches of the shaft. Then I cleaned the hosel and inserted a new shaft. I was ready to go. Sometime later, the same thing happened again: the shaft broke at the same spot one inch above the hosel. I thought to myself there has to be a better way; how can I keep the shaft from breaking in the same spot? The shaft is hollow and it is weak at the lowest point. It takes a lot of abuse when it strikes the ball.

I figured out a way to strengthen the shaft at the bottom. I took a solid steel round rod that fit inside the lower part of the shaft. I cut it about four inches long and glued it inside the shaft. After drying, I glued the shaft into the hosel. Now I never have to worry about the head leaving the shaft again. No question about it, I made the club a little heavier at the bottom, but I was getting more yardage on my drives. Overall, it worked out really well for me.

When the golf companies came out with the new monster drivers, everyone had to go from a two inch tee to a two and a half inch tee because of the larger face on the club. Rather than buy these new tees, I decided to make my own. After trying different ways, I finally came up with a solution. I cut a rubber golf grip two and three eighths of an inch from the top. I inserted a metal washer at the bottom, then inserted a quarter-inch bolt one and three quarters inches long through the bottom of the grip. I inserted another washer on the other side. I screwed a nut into the bolt and filed down the end of the bolt to a point. Next, I cut a wooden handle eight inches long and tapered the bottom to fit inside the open portion of the grip. When teeing up, you can push the handle with the rubber grip inside right into the ground, then remove the handle, put the ball on top of the rubber tee, and you are ready to swing.

I enjoy repairing broken appliances and broken furniture, and each year I refinish my kitchen cabinets. They look new, and the cabinets have a nice lacquer smell to them. Occasionally when some of my neighbors and friends need some help with a piece of furniture, I do the job for them and they are very grateful. I enjoy doing work for a friend; it's a good feeling if I can fix or repair something for them.

At Greenbriar Woodlands each spring, they start the golf season on March first, weather permitting. We also go to various outside golf courses in the area. The swimming pool usually opens around Memorial Day weekend. Our own VFW Post No. 8885 marches in their parade each Memorial Day and Veterans' Day. The many clubs and residents also honor our vets by marching, too. For me, looking at all the World War II veterans and the veterans of other wars, smartly dressed in their gray trousers, white shirts, red ties, and blue blazers, along with their VFW military cap, certainly makes me proud to have been fortunate enough to participate in something so vast that it changed the entire world. The sad thing about Memorial Day is that each year we have fewer and fewer World War II veterans.

When I received my discharge from the army in Heidelberg, Germany, I never received any of the medals that were awarded to me. Personally, I didn't care about the medals. I was just happy to be separated from military duty. It was a three-and-one-half year adventure that I will always remember. I have never asked the army for those medals. I always knew that if I wanted them, I could receive them. Who knows? Maybe someday before I leave this world, I just might request them.

I brought home someone that no medal would ever top, my Irene. She is the best thing that ever happened to me, just meeting and falling in love with my *fraulein*. I wondered if she made the right decision to leave everything behind to join me in a new life in America. She has always told me that she never regretted her decision to spend the rest of her life with me.

Greenbriar Woodlands Bocce Championship.
That's me on the left with my fellow teammates Gladys More,
Lou Paciello, and Frank Sasso. However, we did not win

Our 60th Anniversary

Our children and our grandchildren could not all get together to share in our sixtieth wedding anniversary because of different commitments, but they promised Irene and me that we would all be together in the near future to celebrate this very special anniversary and good fortune. Irene and I shared our own toast on June 7, 2007. We both realized how fortunate and lucky we had been to share these sixty years together. Even at times when things did not look too promising for the two of us, we prevailed. It was a long journey, starting at the bottom of a hole and building a ladder rung by rung, seeing and taking advantage of different opportunities until we were able to climb to the top and out of the hole.

Since I've retired, I play golf quite often, and through the years my handicap has gone up and up. My son once asked me if I ever shot my age. (That is, if my age was eighty and I shot an eighty or better when playing, that would be shooting my age.) When I was eighty-four years old, our golf group went to play at a course called Pebble Creek in Monmouth County. We were six foursomes, and our tee-time was 12:30 p.m.

It was a shotgun start. There were other golfers there from different communities in our area who were also playing in the shotgun start with our group. In fact, there were more than seventy-two players, which is four to each hole. So our guys had to double up on holes with the other groups. In a shotgun start, each foursome tees off at a different hole, from number one to eighteen, all at the same time. One foursome at each hole is a total of 72 players. To double up, each hole has an "A" team. If my foursome starts on hole number ten, and there's a second foursome with us, the second team is called the 10A team. They would start to play immediately after my starting team (the 10 team) tees off.

Because we were all seniors, the course superintendent said that all the golfers had to tee off from the gold tees, which are the seniors' tees. When my foursome played that course, we usually teed off on the white tees. Therefore, I had a great advantage on this round because the gold tees are ten to forty yards closer to the hole than the white tees. It was a lot easier playing from the gold tees. From holes ten to eighteen, I played a great nine.

From holes one to nine, I had a few bad holes, but I knew I had a chance of shooting my age. When the scorekeeper added all the strokes for the entire eighteen holes, he told me, "Lou, you shot your age, eighty-four."

What a great feeling it was to be able to tell anyone who would listen that I shot my age. Again, I have to say that playing from the gold tees gave me a great advantage. I can't imagine shooting an eighty-four from the white tees. Still, being almost eighty-five years old at that point, I think it was quite an accomplishment. When I spoke to Greg on the phone and told him about it, he said he always thought that I could do it.

While playing at the Beylea Golf Course in Toms River at the age of eighty-seven years, I did it again. I shot an eighty-six, which felt great. So as long as I can play the game, I am happy.

On Thursdays, we old-timers play from the gold tees. If only I could putt better, I know I would have a lower score. It's a mental thing, but when I get over the ball to putt, especially if it's within a few feet of the cup, I get so uptight that I usually miss the cup. I can't understand why it happens, but I do know that I have a lot of nervous energy, and I guess it follows me even on the golf course. In a way, I guess it's some sort of a blessing. With this energy, I'm always ready to do something, no matter what.

I was at the doctor's office near the end of 2008, and I mentioned to him this nervous energy that I have, especially on the golf course. I asked him if there was anything I could take for it. He said I might have anxiety. He gave me a prescription to take. Since I have been taking this medication, I feel more relaxed. Even playing golf, I don't feel the anxiety like I used to before.

*Irene's 80th Birthday, May 2006 in an upstate New York restaurant.
Left to right: Greg, Lou, Irene, Celia, Irene's niece Christa, and
Christa's husband, who were visiting with us from Germany.*

On Christmas Day 2007, all our children and most of our grandchildren visited with Irene and me except for Andréa and Xavier. They flew to Paris for the holiday and New Year's to visit with Xavier's parents and family. Irene is very happy when our family gets together. On this occasion, we had lots of food with lots of red and white wine. The following day, Irene made homemade ravioli with meatballs and sausages.

In February 2008, my eldest brother Andy passed away in Florida, where he still lived. He would have been ninety-one in May 2008. Now there are only two of us left: my younger sister Minnie and myself. Minnie was eighty-seven years old in August 2011 and I was eighty-nine years old in July 2011. Personally, I feel good. I'm still doing odds and ends around the house, gardening with Irene, walking, exercising, and of course playing golf.

At the end of March 2008, Irene and I invited my children and grandchildren to join us on a cruise to the Caribbean, which included four stops at different islands. We did not get everyone together, but we had Celia, Karin's two daughters, and a friend of theirs. Overall, it was a pleasant cruise.

My Greenbriar Traveling Golf Buddies
L to R: Marty Sanzari, Lou Paciello,
Me, and John Molinari

Lake Placid

Greg wanted to make plans for the family to go to Lake Placid for a week in autumn 2008, which included golf for any family members who wanted to play.

In July 2008, he called me and said he had made the reservations at the Lake Placid Lodge for early October. I tried to get the entire family to go, but my daughter Karin and her husband Tom couldn't make it because of their business at the boardwalk.

We spent four days there at the Lodge, and it was more than I had ever expected. We ate dinner there each night, and one night we reserved the private dining room there called "The Wine Cellar." They treated us like royalty. There were thousands of bottles of wine all around the exterior of the room. We were served small portions of food and a sampling of wine that complemented that food; next, another kind of food and a different wine for that food. Altogether, we had about seven courses like this, different foods and the wines to go with them. I never drank so many different wines at one sitting before. It was an experience that the children, Irene, and I will never forget.

We also played a round of golf there. Greg does not play the game too much. Xavier is just learning it. Billy loves the game. Greg and Andréa took a boat out on the lake one morning. The weather was starting to get colder, which is normal up there at that time of the year. Overall, though, it was a wonderful trip, and we all had a great time. It was well worth it.

Lake Placid Lodge, New York State – Autumn 2008
Standing L to R: Greg, Nina & Billy, Celia, Melissa, Andréa, Xavier
Seated: Irene & Lou

This is why they call it The Wine Cellar.
They have many of these sections around
the outer walls of this room, with the dining room
table in the center. It's something to see.

Counting My Blessings

At this time of my life, I just want to say that I have been a fortunate man. No one could have predicted what my future had in store for me. As a youth, I was somewhat shy, quiet and laid back. It was good that I had three brothers to share this time with. With the war ending in Europe, who would have thought I would meet and marry a young German girl?

It seems that as far back as I can remember, everything in my life has come together like a jigsaw puzzle. Start to put the pieces together one piece at a time, and slowly you begin to see a small portion of the picture. Continue on and on, and the picture becomes clearer and clearer. As you put the last piece of the puzzle together, you see the entire picture before you.

That, more or less, is what my life is all about. How could I have accomplished all my goals on my own? I have told you earlier in my story and I am going to tell you again. I honestly and personally believe that the Lord has always led me to take the right path. I am so thankful and grateful to Him for watching over my family and me. I am not what you would call a religious person, but there must have been something that He saw that made Him watch over and protect me. Everything just seemed to fall into place. Yes, I consider myself to be one lucky guy.

The End of the Story?

This is the finish of my story, but not the conclusion. It will continue on. Irene and I are fortunate to have three good and wonderful children and now four wonderful grandchildren. We both hope we will see the day when we become great-grandparents. Maybe someday soon, now that Celia's daughter Andréa is married.

I just want everyone to know that there is always hope for everyone. Hope is only a word, but we all know what it means. Never give up hope. We have all said it at one time or another, "We hope and pray that everything turns out okay." I remember years ago when Red Skelton had his TV show, and at the end of each program, he would stand before the camera and the audience, raise his hand, wave his fingers, and say, "God Bless." He said those words so sincerely, and they were real and special to me.

Now it's my turn to say my farewell to all. I'm closing with a special picture of Irene and me. We are looking into the camera and saying the same words:

Irene and Lou
"GOD BLESS"

CPSIA information can be obtained at www.ICGtesting.com
Printed in the USA
LVOW041832140912

298880LV00002B/72/P